To Frederick Eckman

Twayne's United States Authors Series

Sylvia E. Bowman, *Editor*

INDIANA UNIVERSITY

Denise Levertov

DENISE LEVERTOV

By LINDA WELSHIMER WAGNER

COLLEGE & UNIVERSITY PRESS · *Publishers*

NEW HAVEN, CONN.

Preface

CATCHING A STREAM at mid-current is difficult. So also is the work of any critic who attempts to evaluate an artist at the fullness of his career. At 43, Denise Levertov is a prolific poet whose work is considered some of the best in America and, consequently, in the world. Her poetry deserves commendation; it also deserves careful analysis—which it is impossible for the chance reviewer, with his limit of fifty well-chosen words, to give. Therefore, I have tried in this book to point out the strengths and weaknesses of Miss Levertov's poems to the present time, 1966, and to indicate trends within the six volumes of her poetry already published. I have tried to avoid predicting future directions for her art, but—admittedly—my confidence in her abilities has colored some of the conclusions in Chapter VII. I would not have undertaken this study had I not felt that I was working with a major poet.

Levertov's own comments about poetry provide much of the source material for this study. I have quoted heavily from her criticism, believing that—at least in this poet's case—there is a valid correlation between theory and practice. Chapter I, then, attempts to summarize Levertov's views on such matters as the role of the poet, the appropriate language for poetry, the use of organic form, and the importance of sound in poetry—and to relate these beliefs to her poems themselves. Chapter II deals with themes which appear to be characteristic of her work. Significant expansion and modification within several of these theme categories is treated in Chapter III.

Chapters IV and V describe what appear to be Levertov's central technical concerns: Chapter IV studies her use of traditional poetic devices (rhythms, assonance) in relation to the sound fabric of the poem. In Chapter V, such components of organic form as structure, line and stanza division, and typographic effects are analyzed. Structural patterns are named. Describing the synthesis of several kinds of patterns within the 1965 "Olga Poems" concludes Chapter V.

Chapter VI studies closely many of Levertov's worksheets as I attempt again to correlate theory with the practice illustrated by successive versions of poems. Chapter VII describes the existing relationship among Levertov's prose and poetry, both early and recent work. It attempts to place her work amid the diverse strains of contemporary art, treating briefly several major poets whose work has had some affect on her own poetry.

My thanks go to Miss Levertov for her cooperation, and for her permission to use the many published and unpublished materials here included. Thanks go also to her former publishers, Lawrence Ferlinghetti and Jonathan Williams; and to her present publisher, James Laughlin. Materials from the Lockwood Memorial Library Poetry Collection, State University of New York at Buffalo, and the Yale University Library Collection of American Literature are used by permission of those libraries, Miss Levertov, and Mrs. William Carlos Williams.

Parts of this book have appeared recently in *The Fiddlehead*, *The Laurel Review*, and *The Massachusetts Review*. I appreciate the co-operation of the editors who have allowed me to reprint.

LINDA WELSHIMER WAGNER

Perrysburg, Ohio

Contents

Chronology

1923   Denise Levertov, born October 24 in London, England, daughter of Paul Philip Levertoff (Russian; Jewish by birth, Christian by conversion) and Beatrice Spooner-Jones (Welsh).

1940   First poem, "Listening to Distant Guns," appeared in *Poetry Quarterly*.

1943-   Served as civilian nurse in and near London.
1945

1946   Publication of first book, *The Double Image*.

1947   Married Mitchell Goodman.

1948   With husband, came to New York. Kenneth Rexroth's *New British Poetry* appeared.

1949   Son Nikolai born.

1950   Returned to Europe with husband and child; lived at Aix-en-Provence and Genoa.

1952   Returned to New York.

1956   Moved to Mexico.

1957   Second book, first from an American publisher, *Here and Now*.

1958   Third book, *Overland to the Islands*. First appearance in *Poetry*.

1959   Returned to New York.

1960   Fourth book, *With Eyes at the Back of Our Heads;* appeared in Don Allen's *The New American Poetry*.

1961   Fifth book, *The Jacob's Ladder;* traveled in Greece and Italy; became Poetry Editor of *The Nation*.

1963   Awarded Guggenheim Fellowship; participated in international poetry seminar at the University of British Columbia; again became Poetry Editor of *The Nation.*

1964   Sixth book, *O Taste and See;* received fellowship to Radcliffe Institute for Independent Study; taught seminar at The Poetry Center, New York; continued as Poetry Editor for *The Nation.*

1965   Received citation and grant from the National Institute of Arts and Letters; fellowship to Radcliffe Institute continued; taught seminars at Drew University and the City College of New York; "Olga Poems" appeared in *Poetry;* Jonathan Cape published *The Jacob's Ladder* in England.

1966   Taught courses at Vassar; continued work on her collection of prose and her seventh book of poems.

The poet, as a man and citizen, will love his native land; but the native land of his *poetic* powers and *poetic* action is the good, noble, and beautiful, which is confined to no particular province or country, and which he seizes upon and forms wherever he finds it.

—GOETHE

Denise Levertov

CHAPTER *1*

'The Gods Die Every Day'

I *"Illustrious Ancestors" and Other Beginnings*

The Rav
of Northern White Russia declined,
in his youth, to learn the
language of birds, because
the extraneous did not interest him; nevertheless
when he grew old it was found
he understood them anyway, having
listened well, and as it is said, 'prayed
      with the bench and the floor.' He used
what was at hand—as did
Angel Jones of Mold, whose meditations
were sewn into coats and britches.
      Well, I would like to make
thinking some line still taut between me and them,
poems direct as what the birds said,
hard as a floor, sound as a bench,
mysterious as the silence when the tailor
would pause with his needle in the air.[1]

NOWADAYS one seldom judges any person by his ancestors, no matter how "illustrious" they have been. "Illustrious Ancestors" is, however, a good introduction to the poetry of Denise Levertov, regardless of the attention it gives Angel Jones and the Rav of Northern White Russia. It is characteristic of Levertov's work because it is written in "organic form"; it makes use of ostensible fact to lead the reader into broader concepts; and it deals with subjects of deep interest to the poet, poetry (and the qualities that make it good), and people (and the qualities that make them memorable). As Levertov's use of the similes late in the poem shows, these sets of qualities are often interrelated. Such parallels occur not so much because Levertov sees all life in terms of her art, but because she sees poetry in terms of all life. The difference is significant; it may well separate Levertov from many of her contemporaries.

Poetry to Levertov is not iconoclastic. The poet does not withdraw from life in order to practice his art. In fact, she defines the poem as "that which is shared" with the reader—be it an emotion, a scene, an occurrence, or other less specific impressions.[2] The poem, however, has never only this single effect. Its importance as an art form, and as a part of man's life, lies in the fact that it has the power "to capture and exalt the total mind."[3] Even when a poem appears to be a literal description of an object, its scope is broadened through implication.

Considered graphically, the poem seems to Levertov to be a three-dimensional figure, a "mystery" so far as analysis is concerned. There are many techniques which ordinarily are employed in writing the successful poem, but these methods do not insure its creation. In other words, the poet who begins with craft and works toward the poem is likely to fail, for he cannot build the poem. That is an entity in itself, and as such it comes to the poet. The poet may literally be a "maker," but he does not make the poem. He discovers it. As Levertov writes, "I believe the poet must be both: inspired seer and craftsman." The idea is false that "any living substance has come into being by the operation of the conscious logical mind alone. Poetry comes into being only if the unconscious yields up its riches."[4]

In her poetic theory, Levertov emphasizes again and again the poet's need for receptivity, for attention instead of intention. The poem must arise naturally; it cannot be forced. Yet the poet must be aware that the poem exists, and must give his energy to seeing his surroundings; for it is from these surroundings that the poem at least begins. Giving one's attention is a vital part of the poetic process; it is a means of realizing present experience, in which all art must be rooted. Here Levertov's philosophy determines her poetic theory, for she believes firmly that experience is not chaos but order—order which has perhaps to be discovered by the attentive artist.

Levetov is very much conscious of the need for poets to be skilled in their craft, but she also realizes that the poem depends for much of its impact on theme. With her belief in the actual having been verified through years of seeing good poems work, she writes primarily of the objects, scenes, and experiences of her life—and of her own reactions to that tangible world. As she explained in 1960, "I believe in writing about what lies under the hand, in a sense. I think that one should never sort of look around for subjects . . . . poetry arises out of *need,* out of really having something to say about something that we—that the poet —that I—have actually felt or experienced. Not necessarily in the visual world—the external world—it can be an inner experience— but it must be something true."[5]

Again she writes that the poet creates from "honest necessity, from a deep organic need."[6] He must be truthful; his *saying* must be of importance or else all is sham. In a recent essay the poet criticized Edith Sitwell for her pretension late in life, saying that her later poems fail because Miss Sitwell wrote from what Levertov feels to be a meaningless base: "the later poems seem false, lacking in the very depth they seem to claim so fervently themselves. They are overextended, and any such overextension *inevitably* shows up in the *language* and *rhythm,* the very *substance,* of a poem."[7]

This particular quotation is interesting in that it shows the close relationship that Levertov feels exists between the working parts of a poem—its language and rhythm—and its total effect. The poem is an organism. It must stem from truth, but it must also have proficient care in its growth. Few poems spring whole from the poet's experience. Poetry is a skill, a craft, as well as an art; it brings with it the craftsman's obligations—to learn and improve, to create purposefully. In short, the poet has responsibilities to himself as artist, to his art, and to society in general.

In 1965 Levertov described the personal involvement of the poet, or of any artist: "Engagement with an art makes you live more intensely. The manhole cover is suddenly seen as the entrance to the underworld. Don't be afraid of these realizations, and don't dismiss them as delusions. Poetry is not something that can be kept in a compartment of your life. In a way it makes life harder, because the more you commit yourself to it, the less possible it is to drift through your years half awake."[8]

Key words in this statement, it seems to me, are *intensely* and *harder.* The artist works, not only at his writing but at all phases of his living. His deep interest in his life demands an energy and a concentration that many people seldom realize. Levertov also feels that, although the poet must participate in and observe the life around him, he must not exploit either his experiences or himself: he must not use his life primarily as material for his art. Neither should he induce physical sensations through drugs or other sensory affectors. He simply—but intensely—lives, taking naturally from life's happenings. What Levertov demands is that the poet know his world and his language, regardless of how much effort is required; for it is only through accurate knowledge that he can write meaningfully.

The poet's responsibilities to the poem are implied in "Illustrious Ancestors." The poem is to be carefully made: "direct as what the birds said" (clear, immediate, natural, despite all the polish necessary to make it direct); "hard" and "sound" (intense rather than digressive). It is also to be "mysterious," a term suggesting her belief in the subconscious as creator, in the poet as vehicle for the passage of the poem. Levertov feels that the mystery inherent in poetic creation parallels the mystery of all life—which the poem itself ultimately reflects. That Angel Jones, the meditative tailor of this particular poem, was a mystic is also significant to the reference.

Levertov's belief in the inexplicable also influences her poetic themes, for she maintains that nothing lies outside the province of the poet. He must be "greedy" and "self-indulgent"; he must include whatever he considers relevant, even though materials may seem trivial in an objective sense. The poem should be like a Renaissance portrait, filled with detail and color, re-creating not only the subject but also the poet's reaction to it.[9] Levertov sees the poems of Hilda Doolittle as ideal in their projection of this "mystery" of inclusion, particularly in the convergence of present and past.[10] And, as she writes, Chairil Anwar's poetic strength grew from his practice of "continually absorbing anything and everything into his *own* life, his *own* poetry."[11]

The mystic, the dreamlike, the inexplicable, then, all have a role in the poem—provided these extensions are real to the poet himself. The poem should ideally create "beauty"; but that characteristic should be rooted in life, the life of the poet, and not be artificially superimposed on the design of the poem. Again, the most necessary force in the poetic process, Levertov feels, is the poet's genuine personal intensity, his involvement in creating a poem which has meaning—for himself as well as for his reader.

For this reason of personal and social satisfaction, the effort involved in the process of poetry is negligible, in light of the resulting power of the poem:

> The gods die every day
> but sovereign poems go on breathing
>   in a counter rhythm that mocks
> the frenzy of weapons, their impudent power.[12]

Her concept of the poem as "counterforce," as sovereign acting against the disorder of modern uses of life, summarizes the poet's third obligation: that to society. The poem is never to be used as a weapon, even against an unfriendly world; it should instead be a means of reaching that world. In 1960 Levertov affirmed, "I do not believe that a violent imitation of the horrors of our time is the concern of poetry. Horrors are taken for granted. Disorder is ordinary. People in general take more and more in their stride; hides grow thicker. I long for poems of an inner harmony in utter contrast to the chaos in which they exist. Insofar as poetry has a social function it is to awaken sleepers by other means than shock."[13]

This statement gives an important insight into Levertov's character. Perceptive as she is, disappointed as she may be at times with elements of contemporary culture, Levertov would never have written a "Howl" of protest like Allen Ginsberg's.[14] She approaches her milieu positively. Her concept of experience as a revelation of basic order grows from her belief in a systematic universe and in the poem as an orderly re-creation of it. Because the poem as an art form has this inherent design, it cannot merely reflect chaos. Surrounded by an apparently formless society, the poem yet finds order in the reader's mind because of an inviolable "inner harmony." As Frederick Eckman wrote of Levertov's work in 1963, "it is not a poetry of doom. Miss Levertov is more often quietly joyous, shaping the small delights, beauties, and sorrows that are emblems of the human condition."[15]

A somewhat different emphasis is given in Kenneth Rexroth's comment that Levertov is the best of contemporary writers, partially because "she is more civilized." She has "what Ezra

Pound calls culture. . . . She is securely humane in a way few people are anymore. . . . Certainly this is humanism older than the Renaissance, so well founded that it penetrates every bit of life. This is far from the humanism of Sigismondo Malatesta or even Henry Luce—it is more like Lao-tse. If it is really absorbed and manifest in an individual it becomes a rare thing, wisdom. I don't need to labor the point that there exist practically no wise poets nowadays and few for the last two hundred years."[16] Rexroth's enthusiasm has set the tone for much criticism of Levertov. Most readers do recognize the humanity in her writing; they respond to her obvious love of nature, her respect for individual man, her enthusiasm for life—all themes treated in subtle, singing lines.

Conversely, Levertov has her harsher critics, those who say her subject matter is too mundane to be "poetic," her expression too flat to be "musical." One critic concedes that she says what she has to say "gracefully," but his contention is that she "has little reason for saying anything."[17] And so she is censured for the very themes that many readers praise, as Thomas Parkinson does, for being "genuine and moving."[18] This divergence of opinion is to be expected in a field so much dominated by individual taste; it is even more likely to occur when the artist is of one sex and most of her critics of the other. Perhaps the most significant comment that can be made about Levertov's critical position today is that nearly all her readers agree that she is a "serious" poet, a truly able writer, and that her work improves as she continues writing. One can scarcely ask for a stronger consensus midway in a poet's career.

For any contemporary reader, the temptation to classify an artist is great: there are many existing "schools" with their appropriate clichés. Levertov is usually considered a member of the Olson group, along with Robert Creeley, Robert Duncan, and various minor figures. Charles Olson, who gives his name to the group, writes poetry unlike that of any of his so-called followers. In fact, that may be the criterion for being an "Olsonite" —that one's poetry is one's own. Creeley's work, for example, is very much different from Duncan's, just as Levertov's is far from that of any of the others in the group. Admittedly, these poets are united by certain theoretical beliefs, but very loosely. The personal association has been close, particularly between

Olson and Creeley and Duncan and Levertov; but it seems to be founded more on mutual respect for poetry than on similarities among the poems produced. So long as the concept of school is defined, then, as a very easy joining of alliances, Levertov may properly be located within the Olson group.

A broader designation used by some critics is "the Black Mountain school." Black Mountain College in North Carolina was very influential in the arts during the 1950's, when Olson was rector and teacher, Duncan a teacher, and Creeley a teacher and editor. Most of the people so grouped today were never on campus, however; they were published in the school's journal, *Black Mountain Review*. Consequently, the term is so inclusive as to be nearly meaningless.

Another means of describing Levertov's work is to label her a follower of William Carlos Williams. This phrase is, again, too broad to be significant. With his insistence on natural speech rhythms and a reasonably concrete image in the poem, Williams has influenced nearly every modern poet. But ironically, although Levertov greatly respected Williams and greatly admired his poetry, she may well be closer artistically to Wallace Stevens and Hilda Doolittle with her use of sound patterns and subtle rhythms (see pp. 137-38).

Some few readers who categorize all free verse as "Beat" poetry will place her with the Beatniks. Variously as this term has been used in the past decade, in no way does it apply to this poet—socially, philosophically, or artistically.

Perhaps the only accurate categorization so far possible is that of Ralph Mills, Jr., who in 1962 coined the phrase "poetry of the immediate." Mills feels that poetry like Levertov's must be distinguished from that of the early twentieth century, weighted by the "heavy freight of symbolism and external knowledge"—as well as from that of poor craftsmanship. He defines "poetry of the immediate" as that work which signifies "the complex of relationships between the poet and what is close at hand in her *personal* experience. The things, the happenings, the thoughts which are personal events in themselves—everything that constitutes the circumference of the poet's life as an individual—turn into the center of poetry."

Mills also sees the assumption of this source of material for poetry as a shift in poetic rationale: "the literary enterprise should concentrate on assigning judgment and worth to the particularities of their lives within the limited range of individual observation and knowledge. If such writing lacks ambitious scope, it compensates by a penetrating and scrupulous honesty." The poem, also, assumes a newly defined role in becoming "an instrument of personal measure, of tests and balances, estimating and preserving the valuable in the teeth of a public actuality that grows day by day more hallucinatory and unreal."[19]

The result of most of this classification has been a continual misjudgment of Levertov's poetry. Critics say her poetry is good; they do not explain why. They rely on the assumption that it must be adequate because Levertov is an Olsonite, and the members of the Olson group are writing the strongest poetry in the world today. Yet readers must think of poets as individuals, and read each poem with an eye to its distinctive characteristics. Perhaps the wisest approach is that of poet James Wright who admires Levertov's poetry, but describes it as "separate from any school."[20]

Regardless of classification, then, Levertov is now recognized as an able poet, as well as a humane one. It is in connection with this latter qualification that I feel a note about her parentage and childhood to be relevant.

Although Levertov considers herself an American poet, she was born in England—Ilford, Essex, 1923—of Welsh and Russian-Jewish parents. Her mother was descended from the second character mentioned in "Illustrious Ancestors," Angel Jones of Mold, the mystic tailor. Her father, Paul Philip Levertoff, was descended from the noted Hasid, Schneour Zalman, "the Rav of Northern White Russia." While in Königsberg preparing for the life of a rabbi, Levertoff became a Christian; and, from the age of eighteen, he devoted his life toward the unification of Judaism and Christianity. An ordained Anglican priest, he worked diligently in the theory of his mission by writing numerous books in Hebrew, Russian, German, and English.[21] As Director of the East London Fund for the Jews, he published an important quarterly, *The Church and the Jews.*

Yet, in addition to being a fine scholar, Levertoff also was a practical man. Cognizant of the problem of the European "Christian-non-Aryans," people who had given up Judaism but were social outcasts because of their former religion, he opened a hostel at his Shoreditch (London) parish. From the hostel, refugees studied in England and then took positions overseas. The hostel became increasingly important through the 1930's and 1940's.

As Levertoff saw the Judaic-Christian problem, only an intellectual approach was valid—hence his own scholarship and his insistence on study for the refugees. This faith in learning as a means to solutions established the atmosphere of the Levertoff household. Each member of the family was free to think for himself. The family was correspondingly free from any kind of artificial restraint. Since Levertoff was not a parish priest, there were no social-religious activities in which the family participated; the children were, in fact, never forced to attend services.

It is a reflection of the attitudes of the household, I think, that every member of the family wrote. Denise's mother, Beatrice, wrote a novelette about her husband, as well as doing work with the quarterly magazine. Olga Tatjana, Denise's older sister by nine years, wrote and published poetry and maintained many other artistic interests. Both she and Denise were educated at home by their mother. Denise also learned from the British Broadcasting Company's daily school programs and from outside instruction in art, French, and music. After she was twelve, she spent long hours at ballet school; and with that interest, the daily lessons and study periods at home began to taper off, although outside lessons continued. In addition, she read history each day and spent many hours (as she recalls, "voluntarily") at Victoria and Albert Museum and at the National Gallery. The evacuation of her ballet school (1939) put an end to her formal education.

No attempt at summarizing Levertov's studies would be complete without mention of the hours her mother and father spent reading aloud—to each other as well as to other children. Among the stories and novels Levertov remembers hearing are those of Hans Anderson, Beatrix Potter, Andrew Lang, Willa Cather, Dickens, Thackeray, Jane Austen, Trollope, George Eliot, Scott, Tolstoy, Conrad, and the Brontës. During the same years, she and Olga were reading to each other the poems of Stevenson, Tennyson, Keats, Wordsworth, and Auden; and Paul Levertoff was telling the Hasidic legends that figure in his daughter's recent poetry.

Hasidism, as the movement was written of by the late Martin Buber, is perhaps more familiar to our world than it was to England in the 1930's. In Buber's preface to *Tales of the Hasidim: Early Masters,* he describes the belief as "joy in the world as it is, in life as it is, in every hour of life in this world, as that hour is . . . hasidism shows men the way to God who dwells with them 'in the midst of their uncleannesses.' . . . It had nothing to do with pantheism which destroys or stunts the greatest of all values: the reciprocal relationship between the human and the divine, the reality of the I and the You which does not cease at the rim of eternity."[22]

That the influence of Hasidism is important to Levertov is clear from this 1964 comment: "Hasidism has given me since childhood a sense of marvels, of wonder. . . . The Hasidism were a little bit like the Franciscans; although in both movements there was also a very great strain of asceticism, yet along with it there was a recognition and joy in the physical world. And a sense of wonder at creation, and I think, I've always felt something like that. . . . I think that's what poems are all about."[23]

As her 1964 poem "Threshold" reaffirms, wonder is allied with the oracular, the mystic, as well as with the physical (here, pulse, hands):

> . . .
> how shall the pulse
> beat out
> that measure,
> under devious
> moon
> wander swerving
>
> to wonder—
>
> hands turn
> what stone to uncover
> feather of broken
> oracle—[24]

One gloss on this concept of wonder is to be found in a recent study of Jungian thought which Levertov admires. The Jungian belief is that "when man loses wonder the images of the inner world lose their life-giving energy. Ritual becomes repetition, symbol only a sign of that which is already known. . . . If a man holds wonder in his heart, the eternal child of new beginnings can live within him, even in old age."[25] So Levertov speaks in "The Thread" of "Not fear/but a stirring/of wonder makes me/catch my breath"; and in "The Illustration" of "wrong turns that lead/over the border into wonder." And complementing the wonder instilled by Hasidism was her mother's deep love for nature (described so vividly in the poem "The Instant"): "My mother's influence was the important early one that made me as a young child *look* at trees, flowers, etc.—all of nature— with love and enthusiasm."[26]

Because of her father's vocation and interests, Levertov met and listened to many famous scholars—conversing in Russian, German, and English. She partially understands Russian and German; speaks French and Spanish; and is conversant with Italian and Welsh. As a poet, she has translated from other languages into English (Lorca, Tsvetaeva, Supervielle; others from Toltec and Indian dialects). One is reminded of Ezra Pound's dictum that the poet must know languages other than his own in order to fully use the rhythms of his native speech.

Levertov briefly describes her early years, during which she began writing secretly at age nine or ten: "We had a house full of books and everyone in the family engaged in some literary activity. Jewish booksellers, German theologians, Russian priests from Paris, and Viennese opera singers, visited the house; and perhaps my earliest memory is of being dandled by the ill-fated son of Theodor Herzl, the great Zionist."[27] From this rich background came the poet who was to write a few years ago, "Certainly I am an American poet, if anything—I know I am not an English one—nevertheless I feel the great English poets belong to me."[28]

II *The Issue of Language*

Readers agree with Levertov's statement—her poems contain nothing unnatural, nothing suspect, to the American reader. She seems to be American in spirit as well as in language. The greatest critical question here, I suppose, is how did she make the transition? W. H. Auden is the best-known example of a British poet who came to America, searching for a new idiom in the vigor of United States culture; yet most readers feel that Auden has failed in his rediscovery. How then did Levertov make the very real stylistic change from the themes and techniques of a young British neo-romantic (as she was called after her first book, *The Double Image,* was published in 1946) to those of a mature, cosmopolitan poet?

In 1940 Levertov published her first poem in *Poetry Quarterly.* Although she had written during most of her childhood ("unfinished serials and poetry"), she had hidden her work. Encouraged by such poets and critics as Herbert Read, Charles Wrey Gardiner, and John Hayward, however, she gave up her reticence (and, incidentally, the painting that had consumed much of her interest). Her first American publication was in Kenneth Rexroth's anthology of young British poets, in which book Rexroth gave her high praise.

Meanwhile World War II brought many changes: Levertov worked in London as a civilian nurse for several years. She spent 1946 and 1947 as tutor, nursemaid, and bookstore employee in France, Switzerland, England, and Holland. In December, 1947, she married Mitchell Goodman, a Harvard student traveling and studying under the GI Bill. After spending 1948 at the Sorbonne and in Florence, the Goodmans came to New York. Although there were more years in Europe and several in Mexico, the family (Nik was born in 1949) has remained in New York but spends summers frequently in Maine. There is no question that it is as a New Yorker rather than as a Londoner that Levertov now writes.

To return to the explanation for Levertov's successful growth into an American poet, perhaps she herself gives the central reason in this statement: "Marrying an American and coming to live here while still young was very stimulating to me as a writer for it necessitated the finding of new rhythms in which to write, in accordance with new rhythms of life and speech."[29] Levertov was twenty-five, "still young"; her earlier writing had been experimental in the sense that all beginning artists' work is—there are no expected patterns for the poetry, within the broad limitations of a general art form or genre. Therefore, she was still receptive to new methods, subjects, and approaches. She could also employ them with no feeling of betrayal to her earlier work. In fact, as I attempt to show in Chapter VII of this book, some techniques of the early work are very much evident in her current poetry.

She was also inherently interested in the "new." She began reading contemporary American authors long before coming to the United States. She describes "finding" William Carlos Williams in a Paris bookstore—first his book of essays, *In the American Grain;* then his poetry. The poetry, however, she recalls, "didn't mean much" to a young English girl—although she had immediately the sense that "this was a poetry that was *going to be* important for me."[30] It is interesting also that, even though Levertov's first book had been published in 1946, it was eleven years before her second collection, *Here and Now,* was published, this one in America. During those intervening years, Levertov was writing, practicing, experimenting. She was working at her art because it needed work to satisfy her own rigorous demands, as well as her changed perspective. No one is more cognizant than Levertov of the craft necessary to poetry; these are the years of her American apprenticeship, required of herself by a young poet who was already recognized as good.

Levertov's letters to William Carlos Williams, the poet whom she admired but didn't at first get too much from, show that these were difficult years artistically. She had "fallow" times; she read voraciously and was too much influenced by what she had read; she was searching for the right techniques. The largest question in her poetics during this period was the issue of language, or more particularly, of the American "idiom."

Diverse as modern American poets are, they nearly all agree they are using the "American idiom," an English very much different from the present language of the British Empire. An approximation of speech rhythms, the use of dialect or colloquial diction, a definite personal sound—these traits are part of most contemporary poets' rationale. Williams was one proponent of the term "American idiom." Because he felt its employment crucial to any poet's success, he often argued with Levertov about her diction. Her reactions to his criticism show the gradual development of her own beliefs about the language of poetry. In 1961 she takes issue with the phrase in question:

> for me, personally, I cannot put the idea of American idiom *first.* For you it has been a focus, almost a mission. But each person must know his own needs. My need and desire is in each poem to find the tone and measure of what I feel, whether the

language, word by word or measure by measure, strikes the reader as "American" or not. That poem you were distressed by, "The Jacob's Ladder," has to be the way it is because *it sounds the way I think and feel about it,* just as close as I can make it. . . .

And I believe fervently that the poet's first obligation is to his own voice—to find it and use it. And one's "voice" does not speak only in the often slipshod, imprecise vocabulary with which one brings in the groceries but with all the resources of one's life, whatever they may be.[31]

Modern readers are, unfortunately, familiar with the worst of the poems written primarily to create a replica of "natural speech." It is apparent from some few of these poems that an overemphasis on one quality has led to neglect of others equally important to the poem. Levertov is suggesting these other qualities in her mention of *tone* and *measure* and in her defense of her own personal idiom. The poet's language may well be an aggregate, so long as it is his own. Initial word choice is a beginning step. Perhaps as important to the total poem are word placement (line division, syntactic inversion, pause designation) and word compatibility (sound patterns, vowel parallels, echo words).

The poem Williams had questioned, "The Jacob's Ladder," illustrates some of Levertov's beliefs about diction:

> The stairway is not
> a thing of gleaming strands
> a radiant evanescence
> for angels' feet that only glance in their tread, and need not
> touch the stone.
>
> It is of stone.
> A rosy stone that takes
> a glowing tone of softness
> only because behind it the sky is a doubtful, a doubting
> night gray.
>
> A stairway of sharp
> angles, solidly built.
> One sees that the angels must spring
> down from one step to the next, giving a little
> lift of the wings:

> and a man climbing
> must scrape his knees, and bring
> the grip of his hands into play. The cut stone
> consoles his groping feet. Wings brush past him.
> The poem ascends.[32]

Much of this poem's total effect depends on the co̲____ ____ ____ subject and, correspondingly, of language between the first stanza and the rest. Levertov begins by describing what the stairway is *not,* and the imprecise word *thing* and the somewhat redundant *gleaming strands* and *radiant evanescence* help to create the vagueness of the imagined stairway. Many readers of modern poetry might feel that these descriptive phrases should be condensed or replaced by more active (subject-verb) constructions (the adjective has never been used so sparingly as in contemporary poetry); yet these phrases are suitable to the reminiscent tone of that individual stanza. The rest of the poem, however, shows that Levertov uses modifiers economically. Description is, in fact, understated, as in "night gray." When adjectives are used, they are effective in several ways. In, for example, "The cut stone," the word *cut* intensifies the sharpness of the stone through its *c-k* and *t* sounds, as well as its shortness. Its position before the first noun also balances that of the only other adjective in the sentence, *groping,* a word important too for its sound. Interestingly enough, the following sentence, like that preceding, has no modifiers. In fact, there are only the two adjectives in the entire stanza.

That the second stanza contains more modifiers shows one important characteristic of Levertov's poetry—her techniques are not arbitrary; they conform to the demands of the single poem, or stanza, or line. In this stanza, sound pattern dominates word choice. The word *stone* in itself is relatively harsh, as could be the poet's description of the actual stairway. Since the first stanza told what does not exist, the reader is prepared for its opposite in the second. The opening line, "It is of stone," could send the poem in several directions; but Levertov uses the long, resonant *o*'s of *rosy, glowing,* and *tone* to ameliorate the initial effect of *stone* when it appears in isolation. As Frederick Eckman has pointed out, the stairway in its rosiness becomes almost human. The stairway is of "sharp/angles, solidly built," but its is seen as kindly, chiefly because of the sound pattern in second stanza.[33]

The use of the qualifying "doubtful, a doubting/night gray" provides interesting content (especially in relation to the rosy stone), as well as a transition to the sharper sounds of the last two stanzas. The bulkiness must be re-created, for it is through the sharpness of the stair that man conceives its reality. The *s* and *l* sounds of stanza three indicate too that the angels, even in their exertion, move more smoothly than does the man, described through such plosive words as *climbing, scrape, bring, grip.*

Ezra Pound's famous tenet, "Dichten-Condensare" (to make poems is to condense), may support objections to lines like "angels' feel that only glance in their tread" or "the angels must spring/down from one step to the next, giving a little/lift of the wings." Levertov eagerly quotes Pound; she also, however, has pointed out that poetry is a paradox: sometimes condensation calls for expansion—of a primary theme or pattern. Condensation is really the elimination of the non-essentials; it is always the total poetic effect that must determine practice. In these particular lines, the thematic attention of "The Jacob's Ladder" is on the movement up and down the stairs. Detail about that movement, then, is relevant because detail carries the major implication. Even the angels must touch, rather than float. Their movement is significant, of course, in relation to man's progress as described in the fourth stanza.

Also, the rhythmic stanza pattern requires a long fourth line, building into the shorter closing of each stanza. Such arrangement is never arbitrary, but the content has helped to create the existing pattern; most of the stanzas do end with a long, rhythmic sentence. This rising and falling rhythm of long sentences interspersed with much shorter ones, as well as the sound patterns and level of diction used throughout, creates a consistent pace within the poem. As in many of Levertov's poems, the pace is dignified; yet its line-by-line variations keep it from stodginess. There is life within its flexibility. This is the issue the poet is raising when she demands that tone and measure (pace) help to determine word choice.

That Williams was not so far from Levertov's way of thinking becomes more evident when one reads his own poetry. Admittedly, some of his poems are very much the product of his concern with speech rhythms, as is "Exercise in Timing":

> Oh
> the sumac died
> it's
> the first time
> I
> noticed it[34]

As Williams' title indicates, the purpose of the poem becomes central here. In this "exercise" Williams was trying to create the American speech rhythm, not to write a necessarily complete poem. "The Jacob's Ladder" is, on the other hand, a very meaningful poem, giving its title to Levertov's fifth book of poetry and serving as a focus of many themes within the book. Similarly, in the excerpt from Williams' long love poem, "To Asphodel, That Greeny Flower," one notices less use of a conversational idiom; in fact, a few of his phrases might seem out of date. But for the pace, theme, and intent of "Asphodel," Williams' word choice is most appropriate:

> If a man die
>   it is because death
>   has first
> possessed his imagination.
>   But if he refuse death—
>   no greater evil
> can befall him
>   unless it be the death of love
>   meet him
> in full career.
>   Then indeed
>   for him
> the light has gone out.
>
> (*Pictures from Breughel*, 179)

As Robert Creeley has summarized, " 'Colloquial' suggests 'common words,' which is not so simply the case; rather, the patterns of the so-called 'usage' follow an idiomatic structure . . . in that sense they do echo a 'spoken' sense of sequence, rather than a 'literary' one—but the individual words are often in no sense 'colloquial.' "[35] And as Levertov has herself said and shown in Part II of "A Common Ground,"

> Not "common speech,"
> a dead level
> but the uncommon speech of paradise,
> tongue in which oracles
> speak to beggars and pilgrims . . .
>
> speech akin to the light
> with which at day's end and the day's
> renewal, mountains
> sing to each other across the cold valleys.

> (*The Jacob's Ladder*, 3)

Admittedly, these are not the words one uses to "bring in the groceries." Neither are they typically "literary"—*dead level*, for example. They are characteristic of Levertov's usage because, again, for this particular poem as a whole—rhythmically and tonally—they are appropriate.

The central point about language in Levertov's poetic rationale, then, is that *any* word is useable so long as it fits the sound and intention of the poem being written: "if you want to use 'thee' and 'thine,' if you want to use abstruse words, if they really are yours in the sense that you know them and feel them to be the most precise words for what you're saying, you have not only a right but an obligation to use them. . . . It's a question of the individual's idiom, of writing in your own language within your own or up to the limits of your own range of vocabulary, not in some preconceived literary language."[36]

This freedom from arbitrary standards stems once again, I feel, from Levertov's reliance on man's subconscious as the source of his poetry. The poet accepts what language comes to him, but he may revise extensively afterward. The initial words are, more or less, a way *into* the poem. The good poem is so integrated, Levertov believes, that its single parts will be difficult to identify. It will have a rhythm or pace peculiar to it, and this movement—created by the words and their arrangement—helps in determining word choice. The process is cyclic, if not simultaneous. Consistent, too, will be the tone throughout a poem. Levertov compares this central base with the key tone in music, the "horizon note" of a composition. Without being obvious to the reader, it will underlie much of the poem's effect.

Strangely perhaps, the poet has the least choice in determining that most mechanical-appearing phase of the poem: its visual structure or "shape." Line and stanza divisions must reinforce the already-established tone/pace of the poems. As Levertov writes, "the most important skill (if one can call it a skill, it is so largely an instinct) [is knowing] where to break his lines so as to indicate pace and tone."[37] Arrangement is, then, subordinate to the considerations of the total poem. It is only a means to the whole effect intended.

As Levertov's statement once again implies, no matter how well the poet knows the rules of his art, no matter how good a technician he is, he must be guided in his work by the inexplicable "power of poetry." She quotes this comment of Dylan Thomas: "'The best craftsmanship always leaves holes and gaps in the works of the poem so that something that is *not* in the poem can creep, crawl, flash or thunder in.'"[38] And, as she describes the poetic process in her 1960 credo:

> I believe poets are instruments on which the power of poetry plays.
> But they are also *makers*, craftsmen: It is given to the seer to see, but it is then his responsibility to communicate what he sees, that they who cannot see may see, since we are "members one of another."
> I believe every space and comma is a living part of the poem and has its function, just as every muscle and pore of the body has its function. And the way the lines are broken is a functioning part essential to the poem's life.
> I believe content determines form, and yet that content is discovered only *in* form. Like everything living, it is a mystery. . . .[39]

The mystery described in the poem "Illustrious Ancestors" again makes entrance, with the poem given as a means of exploring that mystery. Or, as Levertov might say, the poem serves as a "Jacob's ladder" into those areas of rich, humane perception— for men and angels alike.

CHAPTER 2

'Branching a New Way'

I *The Rationale of Theme*

SO FAR AS theme is concerned, the two poems quoted in Chapter I are characteristic of Levertov's poetry. In both "Illustrious Ancestors" and "The Jacob's Ladder" her subject matter is of deep personal concern. The craft of the poem is one of the subjects of the former poem; but more dominant in both is her depiction of the admirable qualities in man. Both the Rav of Northern White Russia and Angel Jones combine the practical and the spiritual. The Rav's prayers are rooted in reality: "He used/what was at hand"; so too did the tailor. Perceptive and aware of surroundings, the Rav learned much from "having listened well." Yet he has had consistent direction, as does man of "The Jacob's Ladder." Again, man is confronted with the reality in the physical harshness of the stone stairs, yet the poet implies that his spiritual-esthetic purpose dominates his thought: "The cut stone/consoles his groping feet." These heroes, then, have much in common—awareness, direction, sensitivity, perseverance.

There are many such men in Levertov's poems. Contradictory as the statement may seem, mankind is her most common "objective correlative." Each man is usually representative of a broader quality or situation, as well as being a distinct character in himself. The "rainwalker" is an exponent of amused tolerance; the blind man, of surety wise enough to accept help.

Levertov's convictions about what the themes of poetry should be—and the sources for them—are best summarized in these quotations from her recent writing. In 1960 she quotes Ibsen: " 'The task of the poet is to make clear to himself, and thereby to others, the temporal and eternal questions.' "[1] She believes that making the poem is a process of self-education or, perhaps better, self-exploration. Because the subjects from life are complex, they need to be viewed from many perspectives.

> Life is no less complex and mysterious than it has always been. That we dwell in enormous cities, and invent and use astonishing machinery, does not simplify it, but continually reveals the dissolution of limit after limit to physical possibility. Our still tentative awareness of the great gulfs of the unconscious, in constant transformation like the marvellous cloudscapes one sees from a jet plane, must surely lead to awe, not to supposed simplicity. Therefore if our poetry is to seek truth—and it must, for that is a condition of its viability, breath to its lungs—then it cannot confine itself to . . . direct statement, but must allow for all the dazzle, shadow, bafflement, leaps of conjecture, prayers and dream-substance of that quest.[2]

She also describes poetic themes as "matters of the greatest importance to everyone," those concerning "the life of the soul, the interplay of psychic and material life."[3]

It may be somewhat surprising to find this emphasis on soul after the recent poetic allegiance to things—surprising, but not inexplicable. Her statement here has to do with aims rather than with means. When William Carlos Williams wrote that poets should find "no ideas but in things," he was writing about the means a poet was to use to express his thought. He wanted the poem to be vividly concrete, to work through the actual objects of a culture and not to lose its readers in vague abstractions. A poem about a lonesome dog can say a great deal about man's essential separateness; the "thing" is the dog, but its description focuses attention on the intended theme, which may be much broader. Levertov herself elaborated on Williams' famous phrase: that he meant "no ideas left hanging where only the intellect can grasp them; i.e., to use ideas as raw material in poetry, one must make them sensuously present to the imagination, whether by way of the eye or the ear—any means that will work."[4]

Despite her sympathy with Williams' insistence on using the actual, "things" are seldom the primary sources for Levertov's themes. Most of her poems stem from personal experiences—the poem begins not with the object seen in isolation, but with the object *in relation to the poet.* "The Sage" is not about a cat; it is about a cat in the midst of actions which are interpreted by the empathetic poet. Even in poems like "Five-Day Rain," which begin as if they were objective descriptions, the feeling of the poet as a result of the observation is the experience, the major impression of the poem. Levertov's total body of poetry is illustration for her statement that "fragments of experience are in fact the content, the inevitable subject, of poems."⁵ Yet, the use of experience is more than a simple retelling, for the poet's aim should be much greater than narration. For example, Levertov admires greatly this comment of Cid Corman's, that the poem is to be concerned with " 'Not experience thrown as a personal problem on others but experience as an order that will sing to others.' "⁶

Making the poem, then, is never a process of simple observation. The poet must be more involved—emotionally and psychically—than an observer usually is. In demanding this greater inclusion of self, Levertov is like Allen Ginsberg, Robert Creeley, and other of her contemporaries who believe that without real involvement the poet writes only mockeries of poems. Wordsworth's "Preface" has come into its own after years of pretended "objectivity." As Levertov wrote in 1962, the poem must begin with an experience, "a sequence or constellation of perceptions and/or conceptions; and these must be of sufficient interest, felt by the poet intensely enough, to demand of him the act of translating them into words, of giving them their apotheosis into language."⁷

Levertov's poetry shows how firmly rooted in experience the themes of her work are. In *Here and Now,* for example, she moves through New York City: Jackson Square, Hudson Street, Central Park. She plays with her child; she visits galleries; she writes. The life is somewhat bleak; it is occasionally over-dramatized; but it is unmistakably real. Similarly, many of the poems in *With Eyes at the Back of Our Heads* (1960) reflect her life in Mexico, her dissatisfaction amid its beauties, her desire for change. Several other poems trace the decision to return to New York, the actual trip back, and the arrival and re-adjustment. Arrangement, as well as content, clarifies her intention.

Except for a few poems based on significant lines from another's work, her poetry comes largely from actual happenings, often very personal happenings: quarrels, enjoyment of beauty, memories, admiration, love, disgust, pleasure in the physical senses, grief. "Terror" illustrates that the source of the emotion portrayed within the poem can remain obscure; the emotion itself—its re-creation through carpet dust, hard-floors, and physical illness—is the dominant theme:

> Face-down; odor
> of dusty carpet. The grip
> of anguished stillness.
>
> Then your naked voice, your
> head knocking the wall, sideways,
> the beating of trapped thoughts against iron.
>
> If I remember, how is it
> my face shows
> barely a line? Am I
> a monster, to sing
> in the wind on this sunny hill
> and not taste the dust always,
> and not hear
> that rending, that retching?
> How did morning come, and the days
> that followed, and quiet nights?
>
> *(Eyes,* 36)

This is not to say that poetry should be a showcase for the poet's feelings, that it should be cathartic or purgative in effect. It should not be emotion recollected in tranquility, but emotion distilled from the personal, crystallized into the immediately meaningful. Art permits that, although the poet may write from an apparent first-person point of view, the poem can remain free from the sentimental overwash of some autobiography. The best of poets may write about tenderness, joy, hesitation—qualities he has seen through knowing children; but the reader will probably never know from his poems that he has children. The poet is reticent about the details of his own life, not because they are irrelevant but because they are usually submerged in the larger impact of the working poem.

The poet must, however, be open. Levertov insists that, because the making of poetry is partly a subconscious process, the subconscious must be free to move at will through all resources extant. As a result, the poet's work will be of a piece, related through characteristic themes and reactions to them. Only as the character of the poet changes will the themes of his poetry. Necessarily, single poems coalesce into groups—about nature, or death, or poetry itself. And usually, once the self-consciousness of being a poet has worn off, poems will deal with the subjects most important to the poet. Such is the case with Levertov's choice of theme within her poetry.

One concern central to her work is that of living life to the fullest, within the confines of personal ethics and relationships. With a truly Epicurean perspective, Levertov believes that only life experienced completely can enrich man. This concept is the major theme of *O Taste and See* (1964), the title poem of which begins: "The world is/not with us enough/O taste and see." Such emphasis is not new for Levertov. In "The Part" she had admitted:

> my hair rises
> to see your living life
> tamped down . . . .
>
> there, where you live,
> live:
> start over,
> everyman, with
> the algae of your dreams
>
> (*The Jacob's Ladder*, 6)

Beginnings may be small; life may be ordinary; but man must "move deeper into today." In the words of one of her few heroines, "a woman with crooked heels,"

> " 'You know, I'm telling you, what I love best
> is life. I love life! Even if I ever get
> to be old and wheezy—or limp! You know?
> Limping along?—I'd still . . .' "
>
> ("February Evening in New York," *Eyes*, 31)

The failure of "The Old Adam" is his apathy, his lack of aware-ness—"life/unlived, of which he is dying/very slowly"; the promise of the young poet is the fact that his life is "opening, fearful, fearless/thousand-eyed." In this latter poem, "Sparks,"

Levertov includes lines from Ecclesiastes and "The Book of Delight" to state her own convictions:

> Whatsoever thy hand
> findeth to do, do it with thy might . . . .
>
> Prepare for this world as thou
> shoulds't live forever.
>
> (*O Taste,* 15)

As the poet commented during a 1963 reading, this poem relates to "being where we are and still doing all we can."[8]

Her confidence in the value of present life stems partly from her assumption, as has been noted, that the world is orderly: that it moves by plan in balanced, harmonious dignity. Man, animal, spirit—all partake of this great order, an order of which nature itself is the best revelation. Levertov nowhere details her concepts, but she does write of them: "The religious sense—pantheism—the impulse to kneel—seems to me basic human reality . . . the kind of Christianity George Herbert wrote about. . . . At the same time I feel with Thoreau that 'The love of Nature and fullest perception of the revelation which she is to man is not compatible with the belief in the peculiar revelation of the *Bible.*'"[9]

Several of her poems show that she looks with admiration to the pre-Christian world of the Greeks.

> We sigh—or I do—for the days when whole cultures were infused with noble simplicity; when though there was cruelty and grief there was no ugliness; when King Alcinous himself stowed the bronze pots for Odysseus under the rower's benches; when from shepherd's pipe and warrior's sandal to palace door and bard's song, all was *well-made.* . . . Our age appears to me a chaos and our environment lacks the qualities for which one could call it a culture. But by way of consolation we have this knowledge of power that perhaps no one in such a supposed harmonious time had: what in the greatest poets is recognizable as Imagination, that breathing of life into the dust, is present in us all embryonically—manifests itself in the life of dream—and in that manifestation shows us the possibility: to permeate, to quicken, all of our life and the works we make.[10]

Man still has the power to realize himself fully. Levertov's emphasis on self (which several critics have seen as a thematic limitation) is consistent with her admiration for the natural, harmonious world and for man as a part of it. It is this man—sensitive, aware, natural—that figures in Levertov's poetry; and he is usually viewed in relation to nature. In fact, one might say that her poems as a group re-create a world strangely unpeopled.

Her consistent emphasis on nature may appear artificial to some readers because she is by location a "city poet," living as she does in the heart of New York City. It is in keeping with her view of life, however, that she sees natural beauty from apartment rooftops, in the dust of streets in springtime, in a small child's wandering glance toward the sky. The dominant impression of her poem, "February Evening in New York," for example, is not that of city bustle; it is rather of "iris blue" winter air and

> Prospect of sky
> wedged into avenues, left at the ends of streets,
> west sky, east sky: more life tonight! A range
> of open time at winter's outskirts.
>
> (*Eyes,* 31)

It is interesting that New York is seldom recognizable as a particular city in Levertov's poems; it instead merges with her own microcosm of rural and urban existence. Summers spent in the old Maine farmhouse, years of living in Mexico, youth spent in the suburbs of London—all have provided rich experiences with nature in settings far separate from that of New York City. The poem "realistic" in every detail is not Levertov's aim. It is instead the poem which speaks to a common element in man, regardless of his location. "The Rainwalkers" could be walking through any city; "Coming Fall" could be approaching any locale; the bird in "Flight" could be captured in any room.

Contrary to what has come to be expected of "nature poets," Levertov uses few images of flowers in her poetry. Not flowers or trees but fruits are the basic image in many of her poems. Such an emphasis reveals again an insistence on the richest experience possible, the total commitment: one can admire a flower—he can look at it and smell it. He can also look at and smell fruit, but in addition he can taste it, he can be fed. In "Pleasures," she writes of the physical satisfactions possible:

> Or a fruit, *mamey,*
>
> cased in rough brown peel, the flesh
> rose-amber, and the seed:
> the seed a stone of wood, carved and
>
> polished, walnut-colored, formed
> like a brazilnut, but large,
> large enough to fill
> the hungry palm of a hand.
>
> (*Eyes,* 17)

Of visual satisfaction alone, Levertov writes, "But these are thin pleasures, to content/the contented." For hunger:

> something
> of endurance, to endure
> a ripeness if it come, or suffer
> a slow spring with lifted head—
> a good crust of brown bread for the hungry.
>
> ("Bread," *Eyes,* 52)

Physical enjoyment comes to be as important to the poet as the esthetic. Her poems indicate that her capacity for both is great. As she insists in "O Taste and See," man must enjoy "all that lives/to the imagination's tongue":

> grief, mercy, language,
> tangerine, weather, to
> breathe them, bite,
> savor, chew, swallow, transform
>
> into our flesh our
> deaths, crossing the street, plum, quince,
> living in the orchard and being
>
> hungry, and plucking
> the fruit.
>
> (*O Taste,* 53)

This collage of abstract and tangible, emotion and food, all serving as nourishment to the physical body (for which death is as routine an experience as crossing the street) is vivid proof of Levertov's intensity. The title also, of the poem and the book, emphasizes the rationale that sensory experience is necessary to live fully. By using the inverted order of *taste* and *see* as it stands in the Bible, she too implies a cause-and-effect condition: because one has tasted, he then can see. Seeing is no longer a matter of merely recognizing external qualities.

An early poem, "Laying the Dust," shows further the inclusion of her love for the natural. The poem begins with a simple happening:

> What a sweet smell rises
>   when you lay the dust—
> bucket after bucket of water thrown
> on the yellow grass.

From this experience, the poet concludes

> Surely when flowers
> grow here, they'll not
> smell sweeter than this
>   wet ground, suddenly black.[11]

Images of soil (expressed usually as *mud* or *ground*) appear frequently throughout Levertov's poems, but they are always related, at least by implication, to her interest in seeds which contain life. The earth figures as the environment of the seed, the home of its nourishment. In "A Ring of Changes," she writes of "Shells, husks, the wandering of autumn seeds," commanding,

> Seed, cling
> to the hard earth, some footstep
> will grind you in
>   (*Eyes*, 37)

Gaining life is seldom easy; finding sustenance is frequently unpleasant. All life must join in creating the new, " 'From thy dung/the red flowers,' says the god." Even the act of poetry springs at times from the earth:

> There in the cold air
> lying still where her hand had thrown me,
> I tasted the mud that splattered my lips:
> the seeds of the forest were in it,
> asleep and growing! . . . .
>
> I bit on a seed and it spoke on my tongue.
>
> ("The Goddess," *Eyes*, 43)

The most vivid use of earth as an image of fertility occurs in "Song for Ishtar." Equating moon with sow and poet with pig early in the poem, Levertov describes "the mud of my hollow" which "gleams/and breaks in silver bubbles." Satisfaction results from the transformation of human crassness, as moon-goddess-poet are finally united: "In the black of desire/we rock and grunt, grunt and/shine" (*O Taste*, 3). This use of the "unpoetic" sow is once again characteristic. A concern with animals pervades her poetry, but not the animals generally associated with poetry. There are to be sure a few dogs, the wise and implacable cat (in early poems), some random birds—but the strongest images are of barnyard and forest animals: the sow, wild rabbits, the "forest bear," tigers, elephants, giraffes, snakes. Her very selection of animals excludes man's influence. These are independent creatures, each of whom has enough wit to exist alone. Even the dogs in the poems are strays, moving in quest, "each step an arrival." Often, too, an animal is depicted as alone: it is *"the* serpent," *"an* armadillo," *"the* lonely white rabbit." Group existence is evidently not basic to Levertov's utopia.

By implication, her admiring descriptions of animals censure man. "Come into animal presence," she directs. "No man is so guileless as/the serpent." The joy to be found in this "holy presence" results from seeing that "no animal/falters, but knows what it must do"; that the animals move in silence, in dignity, having "some intention to pursue."[12] This relation of animals to holiness is to be expected because of Levertov's belief in an orderly world. Animals illustrate the untutored, uncorrupted response to life; therefore, as the world is orderly, so is the animal's life.

As a further statement of her belief in the pervasive natural order, the image of design comes frequently into the poems. "The Tide" moves through design, as does the wind, and also the poet:

> By design
> clear air and cold wind polish
> the river lights, by design
> we are to live now in a new place.

("From the Roof," *The Jacob's Ladder*, 50)

Man, then, can also partake of the holiness of nature, so long as he recognizes the natural pattern and lives within it. As she explains in her recent poem "The Novices," man and boy are called to the forest, not for any formal initiation to life,

> but that they might look about them
>
> and see intricate branch and bark,
> stars of moss and the old scars
> left by dead men's saws . . .
>
> To leave the open fields
> and enter the forest,
>
> that was the rite.
> Knowing there was mystery, they could go.
> Go back now!
>
> (*O Taste*, 57)

Man initiated to the natural beauties, the natural rhythms of life, regains an original insight into life. He approaches a kind of holiness. The keenest recognition comes, however, to the man who leads others to initiation, the artist himself, as she says of the poet in "Earth Psalm,"

> I could replace
> God for awhile . . . .
>
> awhile I can turn from that slow embrace
> to worship *mortal*, the summoned
> god who has speech, who has wit
> to wreathe all words, who laughs
> wrapped in sad pelt and without hope of heaven,
> who makes a music . . .
>
> (*O Taste*, 80)

Increasingly in her more recent poems, Levertov emphasizes the possibilities of sensitive man to recapture a natural harmony. It is not accidental that the most satisfying encounters for the poet take place in natural settings, as in "Eros at Temple Stream." Regardless of geography, however, the poet quotes Rabbi Judah Loew: " 'In some special way every person completes the universe. If he does not play his part, he injures the pattern of all existence.' "[13] She has said that man's world has "no grace like that of/the grass"; she shows, however, that, although the world taken in total may be less than perfect, an individual's life can be filled with grace: "I don't want to escape, only to see/the enactment of rites."

Compassion seems to be Levertov's answer to most present evils. The poem about Greek life, "In Abeyance," describes contemporary culture simply but tellingly,

> we are so many
>   and many within themselves
> travel to far islands but no one
> asks for their story
>
> nor is there an exchange of gifts, stranger
>   to stranger
> nor libation
> nor sacrifice to the gods
>
> and no house has its herm.
>   (*O Taste*, 54)

Man's lack of concern for others is also the theme of one of her strongest poems, "During the Eichmann Trial"—that man does not look, either into others or into himself. Her opening sequence sets forth this explanation for the tragedy of a person like Eichmann:

> He had not looked,
> pitiful man whom none
>
> pity, whom all
> must pity if they look
>
> into their own face (given
> only by glass, steel, water
>
> barely known) all
> who look up
>
> to see—how many
> faces? How many
>
> seen in a lifetime? (Not those
> that flash by, but those
>
> into which the gaze wanders
> and is lost

> and returns to tell
> *Here is a mystery,*
>
> *a person, an*
> *other, an I?*
>
> (*The Jacob's Ladder,* 61)

After a presentation of his crimes, the poet concludes, "Pity this man who saw it . . . he, you, I which shall I say?/He stands/ isolate in a bulletproof/witness-stand of glass,/a cage, where we may view/ourselves, an apparition/telling us something he/does not know: we are members/one of another."

In contrast to the painstaking effort required to truly see and know another person, Levertov presents the facile, meaningless movement of "Merritt Parkway,"

> the humans from inside the
> cars, apparent
> only at gasoline stops
>   unsure,
> eyeing each other
>
>   drink coffee hastily at the
>   slot machines & hurry
> back to the cars
>   vanish
>   into them forever, to
>   keep moving—
>
>   (*Overland,* 6)

II *The Silence-Motion Paradox*

Levertov has said that the essence of poetry, like the essense of life, is paradox. And paradox does run through her descriptions of man. On one hand, she urges man to live to the fullest, to taste, to feel, to see everything possible. This imperative implies motion, activity. Yet in other poems she degrades the movement of activity as escape from the real issues of living. A further parallel (which is also paradoxical) is her insistence on both communication and silence. In "The Park" she presents lifeless people who miss experience because they "turn their heads away," "they talk and delay." Usually, silence is the ideal state, the most expressive of conditions.

Her recent poem "The Breathing" captures the feeling of the slow quiet she so often equates with fulfillment:

> An absolute
> patience.
> Trees stand
> up to their knees in
> fog. The fog
> slowly flows
> uphill.
>   White
> cobwebs, the grass
> leaning where deer
> have looked for apples.
> The woods
> from brook to where
> the top of the hill looks
> over the fog, send up
> not one bird.
> So absolute, it is
> no other than
> happiness itself, a breathing
> too quiet to hear.
>
>   (*O Taste*, 8)

The very slowness of the poem itself (achieved through long vowels and short phrases) builds toward "a breathing too quiet to hear"—sound that exists without acknowledgment, without fanfare, without recognition.

Again and again, the image of silence dominates Levertov's poems. It is used more frequently than any other single motif and in so many different kinds of poems that it appears to be integral to the poet's philosophy. William Carlos Williams had written that silence is fine, "but you do not get far/with silence." Levertov seems to believe that one gets nowhere without it. The paradox inherent in a poet's demanding silence can be resolved through Levertov's definition of that state. In "Silence" she describes a rose wet with morning rain; and then she concludes: "Silence/surrounds the facts. A language/still unspoken." Words beyond words, a sensed rapport. The long poem "A Sequence" explores this contrast between the spoken and the unspoken. The poet speaks "flatly." He must restate what has already been said,

"I had meant to say . . . ," only to have his companion challenge, "That's not enough." He is then forced to answer,

> It's true.
> Nothing
>
> is ever enough. Images
> split the truth
> in fractions. And milk
> of speech is black lava . . .
>> (*The Jacob's Ladder*, 9)

The conversation degenerates into non sequiturs. Only in silences and in "naked laughter, trembling with tenderness and relief" are the two speakers finally united. As the poet concludes in another poem, "The Marriage, II": "Speak or be silent. Your silence/will speak to me."

The height of re-creation of this wordless communication comes within "In Memory of Boris Pasternak." Here a burnet moth at a subway entrance is "a word,/an emanation from him." The most vivid speech comes to the poet through nature—the road into the forest, wild strawberry leaves, a barn—"all/lifts itself, poises itself to speak":

> something is said, quickly,
> in words of cloud-shadows moving and
> the unmoving turn of the road, something
> not quite caught, but filtered
> through some outpost of dreaming sense
> the gist, the drift.
>> (*The Jacob's Ladder*, 33)

"The gist, the drift"—an impression perhaps more meaningful than words could ever be.

When Levertov speaks of the "green silence and apparent stillness" of a living tree, she increases the suggestivity of her use of motion and sound. Because an object is at rest, then, it need not be lifeless. (The silence of death as she describes it is different—"heavy," "thick.") There can be constant movement in any living thing, esthetically as well as physically. "Green silence" implies the ability to create sound. In "A Solitude," she describes two kinds of quiet: one, "the quiet of people not speaking,/some of them eyeing the blind man"; the other, "within that quiet his/different quiet, not quiet at all, a tumult/of images," a "green silence."

From her use of the word "silence," Levertov suggests that silence can go beyond the effectiveness of sound, that it can permit people to truly know what they are seeing and thinking. Silence does not oppose speech; it is both an extension of it and a channel for it. Poems, for example, spring from "the whole/cloth of silence." In contrast, they are seen "leaping from shattered windows" in a world characterized chiefly by "clamor." "The World Outside" depicts existence in which peace (perhaps) accompanies the final silence of dark windows, whereas it had been missing from conversation, music, parties, love, or television.

Silence also characterizes people that Levertov admires. "Old Day the gardener" worked "slow and in silence." The blind man walks quiet, "in a great solitude." The amused acceptance of the rainwalker and his two dogs is silent—not, however, austere or aloof. Silence implies tranquility rather than withdrawal. In contrast, it is the incessant talker who realizes only the narrowest of boundaries.

It is significant to notice one of her technical practices that is relevant to this interest in theme: she seldom uses the device of "conversation" within her poems—as do William Carlos Williams, Robert Creeley, and other poets who are working within "natural speech rhythms." Levertov writes monologues, not dialogues. People are not, however, isolated in her poetry. They do many things together—work, walk, write, observe, make love—but they seldom talk. Their communication is one of action, not words.

Her insistence on tranquility in both movement and sound can be attributed partly, I think, to her growing conviction that some of life's most valuable experiences—including the creation of the poem—stem from the subconscious. All parts of the person must therefore be free to respond to stimuli; receptivity is heightened when distractions are at a minimum. Thematically, this belief is substantiated by Levertov's increasing emphasis on the importance of intuition, fantasy, and dream as means to knowledge. Of the three, dream appears most often in her poetry. At times a vehicle for poetic inspiration, it is also in itself a process of knowing:

as we think an undercurrent
of dream runs through us
faster than thought
toward recognition.

("Matins," *The Jacob's Ladder*, 58)

The dream represents all the untapped resources of the mind, the supra-rational. In "The Tide" she defines dreams as "intelligence of/what pulls at our depths for design." Again, she stresses the pervasive order of life, revealed in man's innermost experience, through dreams.

The mind also has other functions besides rational thought and dream. "A Ring of Changes" describes the awareness of people "not quite awake and so awake/to correspondences." Another means of accurate perception is meditation, as she recounts in "A Letter to William Kinter of Muhlenberg": "mind and heart/gave themselves to meditation/moving deeper/and deeper into Imagination's/holy forest." The bond between artistic fulfillment and concentration or meditation is one of the major emphases in her recent criticism:

Now, presuming as I do that there *is* a form to be found, an inscape that relates the apparently unrelated, or at any rate confusing, multiplicity of awarenesses, the next step is to mediate upon it, to contemplate it. Contemplation—meditation— the words are taken from the religious vocabulary, and surely this is no accident; for we should remember the ritual, sacramental roots of art and realize that the act of creating a work of art is in its nature a celebration of life (even though the work itself may be concerned with death) and that the artist himself has a function not very different from that of the priest or shaman.

The act of art evokes a spirit, and in assuming the existence of a spirit, and the possibility of a transformation by means of that spirit, it is an act of prayer. It is a testimony of that *participation mystique*, that involvement of the individual in a life beyond himself, which is a basic element of religion in the broadest and deepest sense. The poem communicates something more of life to the receiver than he would have without it, and the poet is the mediator or priest in this rite of communion, in which, as in Christian communion, he himself participates also as a receiver. *Contemplation* and *meditation* are words which denote a state in which the heat of worshipful feeling warms the intellect. Their derivation is of interest here: to contemplate comes from templus, temple, "a place, a space for observation, marked out by the auger." Its meaning is not simply to observe, to regard, to consider, but to do these things in the presence of the god. To meditate is "to keep the mind in a state of contemplation" and a synonym for it, a word which comes, comically enough, from a word meaning "to stand with open mouth," is "to muse"—but it is not a meaningless comedy if we think of the word *inspiration,* literally, "to breathe in" and remember, along with that, the common primitive belief that the soul could enter or leave the body by way of the mouth.

As the poet, then, stands open-mouthed in the temple of life contemplating his experience, the first words of the poem come to him—the words which are to be his way in the poem. . . .[14]

Meditation, dream, the spirit—all share in the moment of the poem. Elsewhere Levertov has referred to poetry itself as an "elusive dream," equating it with religious duty and seeing in it one concept of immortality: "Our lives flower and pass. Only robust works of the imagination live in eternity" ("Art," *Eyes,* 72).

As a corollary of this present belief, the essence of poetry—represented traditionally by the figure of the muse—is no longer mystical or fantastic. She sees her muse now as a sacrament of the home, as much a part of the poet as a worn wedding band. Like the gold ring, the muse is unobtrusive but necessary. In earlier poems, the poet had paid visits to an oracular spirit—visits characterized by anguish and physical illness. In her 1964 poem, the muse lives within the poet, sustained by her personal tranquility. Seeing the spirit of poetry as a natural part of the poet is only another substantiation of Levertov's trust in the natural order.

It is partially because of this strong belief in innate order that images of nature have dominated and continue to dominate Levertov's poems. She will probably never outgrow the themes of nature. Many contemporary poets begin their careers writing about nature (because it is beautiful, it is traditional, and it does have a least-common-denominator quality), only to move away from it in their later—and often their best—poems. They turn instead to urban subjects as being more immediately interesting, thinking of the city in opposition to the natural, and choosing between the two. This is not Levertov's attitude. With her poems revealing more and more of her personal beliefs, nature seems to become an even more important source of themes and images, as if Levertov saw the natural within the urban as the origin of whatever order the latter environment maintains.

One might compare the recurrence of her poetic themes to the straggling chain of circles formed by a child learning penmanship. The hand moves slowly, tentatively, on the first oval. As it is completed, another grows from the same point of origin —but there are differences between the two circles. The line of ovals progresses, the figures growing firmer as the child becomes more confident.

So it is with the themes of Levertov's poetry. Two, three, four poems may rise from the same point of origin, with the later poems written moving beyond the first, in skill (usually), inclusion, and implication. For example, "A Ring of Changes" is the second circle; "Terror," the first. Both deal with man's essential loneliness, the limitations of sympathy, the necessity for human relationships. In "Terror," the poet writes of one experience, the observer torn by the conflict between his realization of misery and his inability of sympathize. The "terror" one feels is not evoked because of another person's plight, but because of the poet's recognition of basic human separateness (see p. 39). In "A Ring of Changes," Levertov weaves this theme into a broader pattern of man's relation to nature-life as well as to other men. Lines midway through this poem unite it with "Terror":

> What holds us upright, once we have faced
> immeasurable darkness, the black point
> at our eyes' center? Were we suspended,
> museum butterflies, by a filament, from a hidden nail?
> Has it broken when we begin to
> fall, slowly, without desire?
> (But we don't fall. The floor is flat, the round earth
> is flat, and we stand on it, and though we lie down
> and fill our lungs with choking dust
> and spread our arms to make a cross
> after a while we rise and creep away,
> walk from one room to another
> "on our feet again.")

> *(Eyes,* 40)

By including the direct mention of the cross (only suggested in the shorter poem), she further widens the import of the poem. The later poems "During the Eichmann Trial" and "Into the Interior" could easily be considered extensions of this same thematic base. These poems show that surety does increase with exploration and familiarity. It also does much to convince the reader that her poems are rooted in life, for experience is—in many cases—cyclic. Levertov herself recently compared life's experiences with "a meandering road that frequently loops back almost to the starting point . . . certain events, never exorcised by understanding perhaps, are repeated, sometimes over and over; certain questions are asked, and no satisfactory answer being received, are asked again. But the road is not a ring. At the last it disappears into the distance, as is proper to its nature."[15]

A frequent use of the images and themes of nature as representative of the universe's inherent balance is, then, predictable. It is, however, never repetitious. Each poem has its own "quavers and minims," its own beauty in execution. Late poems like "Claritas" provide good illustration of the possible freshness of these recurring subjects. In "Kingdoms of Heaven" she has written of the poetic process—and the cycles of existence related to it:

> Stir of time, the sequence
> returning upon itself, branching
> a new way. To suffer, pains, hope.
> The attention
> lives in it as a poem lives or a song
> going under the skin of memory.
>
> (*O Taste*, 12)

'A Becoming Aware'

I *Modification within Themes*

IT WOULD BE FOOLISH, however, to assert that one person's attitudes can remain constant throughout a lifetime. Just as man grows and changes, so do the themes of concern to him, although modification might be a more accurate term than change. As Charles Olson has said, men do not so much change as stand revealed. Viewed chronologically, then, the poetry of any honest person should be indicative of (or perhaps, bear witness to) his progress as a human being. Accordingly, there has been expansion within several of these already dominant themes of Levertov's poetry.

One of the most noticeable expansions has been in the poet's depiction of herself. From the wistful bystander of "Gypsy's Window," she has become a sensitive, sensual woman, powerful in her maturity and in her loves. Self-consciousness has given way to a healthily aggressive pride in self, evident in "Earth Psalm," and in her reproof to "Hypocrite Women": "And our dreams,/with what frivolity we have pared them/like toenails, clipped them like ends of/split hair." Or there is the wistful assurance that closes "September 1961":

> But for us the road
> unfurls itself, we count the
> words in our pockets, we wonder
>
> how it will be without them, we don't
> stop walking, we know
> there is far to go, sometimes
>
> we think the night wind carries
> a smell of the sea . . .
>
> (*O Taste*, 10-11)

In 1964, Levertov wrote that the key to personal fulfillment lay in "a becoming aware." Consonant with the title of her last book, *O Taste and See,* this belief not only includes the premise that experience is the source of art/life, but also widens that earlier rationale. She insists that the poet's personal involvement be entire. As she writes of man's duty:

> to be
> what he is
> being his virtue
>
> filling his whole space
> so no devil
> may enter

("Thee Meditations," *The Jacob's Ladder,* 31)

This new honesty, or perhaps new awareness, compels her to reveal facets of personality undisclosed in earlier work. One of the most striking is a "necessary" cruelty, the paradoxical impulse toward both selfishness and self-abnegation. The poem "In Mind" presents the dichotomy which had been described obliquely in "Earthwoman and Waterwoman" and in "Mrs. Cobweb." In "In Mind," however, she speaks not about others but about herself as *persona*:

> There's in my mind a woman
> of innocence, unadorned but
>
> fair-featured, and smelling of
> apples or grass. She wears
>
> a utopian smock or shift, her hair
> is light brown and smooth, and she
>
> is kind and very clean without
> ostentation—
>   but she has
> no imagination.
>   And there's a
> turbulent moon-ridden girl
>
> or old woman, or both,
> dressed in opals and rags, feathers
>
> and torn taffeta,
> who knows strange songs—
>
> but she is not kind.

(*O Taste,* 71)

The same motif underlies "Melody Grundy," who is indifferent to all opinion, and "The Elves" whose company can be known only by a woman who "has that cold fire in her/called poet." In "Three Meditations," written in 1960, Levertov approached this present attitude in the lines,

> There is darkness in me . . . .
>
> Who was it yelled, cracking
> the glass of delight?
> Who sent the child
> sobbing to bed, and woke it
> later to comfort it?
> I, I, I, I,
> I multitude, I tyrant,
> I angel, I you, you
> world . . .

Though effective, this passage strikes me as less honest than the poem "In Mind" because the focus turns away from the poet toward other men—the multitude, the world—and loses itself in generalities. Levertov appears to be using the poet here as an objective correlative rather than as a person in her own right.

Further evidence of this move toward "to be/what he is" is an emphasis on the physical—or, more accurately, the sensual—in such poems as "Losing Track," "Eros at Temple Stream," "The Ache of Marriage," and "A Psalm Praising the Hair of Man's Body." Although her depth of physical feeling was evident in earlier poems, it had never appeared with such consistency. "The Third Dimension," one of Levertov's best early poems, achieved this now-characteristic intensity only through a hypothetical situation:

> Who'd believe me if
> I said, "They took and
>
> split me open from
> scalp to crotch, and
>
> still I'm alive, and
> walk around pleased with
>
> the sun and all
> the world's bounty." Honesty

> isn't so simple:
> a simple honesty is
>
> nothing but a lie . . . .
>
> *(Here and Now, 25)*

Perhaps it is that the poet's appreciation for her readers has broadened. In her later poems, she evidently feels that someone would believe her. And one does—as in the case of the haunting, heavily figurative tone poem, "The Ache of Marriage."

> The ache of marriage:
>
> thigh and tongue, beloved,
> are heavy with it,
> it throbs in the teeth
>
> We look for communion
> and are turned away, beloved,
> each and each
>
> It is leviathan and we
> in its belly
> looking for joy, some joy
> not to be known outside it
>
> two by two in the ark of
> the ache of it.
>
> *(O Taste, 5)*

A clumsy, desperate poem—intentionally, for that is the aching quality of a marriage, a search for communion—transposed into the movements of love rather than its words. This poem is not Levertov's first expression of marriage, but it is one of the first to relate her feelings as woman to the relationship—as ark, as recipient as well as participant. "Song for Ishtar" and "Hypocrite Women" also reveal this newly expressed ethic of the complete woman.

In contrast to this work, most of her earlier love poems were vague, romantic descriptions—as in "The Marriage, I and II." In her 1958 and 1960 collections, however, marriage provided powerful metaphors for poems ostensibly "about" other themes ("A Ring of Changes," "Luxury"), but she seldom wrote about love itself. She came close to evoking this present sensuality in "The Bird" and "To the Snake"—poems not directly concerned with the love relationship. "To the Snake," for example, employs strong physical images to re-create the complete absorption of the artist in his art—an absorption contradicting all logic, "only desiring/to hold you, for that joy,/which left/a long wake of pleasure . . ."

> Green Snake, when I hung you round my neck
> and stroked your cold, pulsing throat
>   as you hissed to me, glinting
> arrowy gold scales, and I felt
>   the weight of you on my shoulders,
> and the whispered silver of your dryness
>   sounded close at my ears—
>   (*Eyes*, 74)

Once the snake has gone, the poet returns "smiling and haunted, to a dark morning." Few experiences are realized more physically than this one is. The long, heavily accented lines enhance the stroking motion used as the basis for the poet's response to the snake. The blending of the *g*, *l*, and *s* sounds lends further motion to the phrases, as in "glinting arrowy gold scales," a motion which underlies the effect of the poem seen as a whole.

Other poems which employ these images of sensuality within a context of resonant, warm vowels are "Song for a Dark Voice," "Resting Figure," and "Love Song" (see p. 88). The lush images of the former poems ("Your tongue has found/my tongue, peonies/turn their profusion towards/the lamp, it is you that burn there") are more subdued in "Love Song," but no less fervent. And the images usually associated with her concept of sensuality—rippling movement, darkness, gutteral sounds, body hair—appear frequently in many of these late poems. Objects from a still life are "rippling/as if with laughter," the old maple groans with "almost unbearable satisfaction," the act of creating a poem is as physical as intercourse.

The greater use of these sensual images may indicate once more that her concept of appropriate sources for the poem has changed. It would seem that she includes more essentially personal responses in these poems; and a reliance on dream, legend, and myth is noticeable. The themes of many poems from *O Taste and See* relate to inner experiences while those from earlier collections are based on external happenings, with the poet appearing more often as observer than as participant. Her interest in her observed subjects is, of course, implied; but it is often not central to the poem. Many of the poems from *The Jacob's Ladder* (1960) stem from her reading. She uses epigraphs from the work of Boris Pasternak, Rabbi Judah Loew, Charles Olson, Henrik Ibsen, D. H. Lawrence, Jules Supervielle, Robert Duncan —all quotations of relevance and interest. The reader senses, however, that in some ways the poems are less immediate than those of the later book. Corresponding with the rationale that a full experience demands physical participation, these poems initiated by reading, in some sense, do lack intensity. It is significant also that one of the weaker poems in *O Taste and See* is "A March," one of the only two poems from that collection stemming from epigraphs.

Because Levertov arranges her books carefully, the order of poems is important. In any collection, openings and closings are usually strong. It is interesting, then, that *O Taste and See* opens with a group of three poems which are admittedly "first draft," and with a fourth which was close to it. Not a word of "Song for Ishtar," "The Elves" or "The Ache of Marriage" was changed after the initial writing; very little was done to "Love Song." For such a conscious artist as Levertov, satisfaction with any poem in its original state indicates a deep trust in those inexplicable creative processes. Similarly, the volume closes with a group of runes which, in the poet's words, "were given me in a dream. In the dream I was a Finnish child of eight or nine who had been given by her teacher the task of writing out these three ancient runes of her people. This is how they went."[1]

Many poems within this last book reinforce Levertov's emphasis on intuitive response. "The Message" from the Spirit of Poetry arrives "out of sea fog" through "a letter in dream." And the message is, fittingly, that the poet remember her personal nature, her inherent powers. In "To the Muse," she concludes that the poet's power is not evanescent, secretive; it is "indwelling," like "a gold ring lost in the house." All the poet needs do to experience her gift is to become aware:

> Be ready with quick sight to catch
> a gleam between the floorboards,
>
> there, where he had looked
> a thousand times and seen nothing.

> (*O Taste*, 27)

The issue of recognition, of personal perception, again becomes central. In "Love Song" and in "Another Spring" the
essence of the poet's strength lies in the ability to see clearly—
and, for Levertov, clarity stems increasingly from intuition. As
she asks in "The Ground Mist,"

> But is illusion
> so repeated, known
>   each dawn,
>   silence
>   suspended in the
> mind's shadow
>
>   always, not substance
> of a sort?
>   (*O Taste*, 40)

In what lies substance, in what lies the real, if not in illusion,
in self-discernment of the real? Who can argue with the poet
when she writes, albeit paradoxically, of human figures "in the
last sunlight, dark on the hill/a fur of gold about their shoulders
and heads, a blur defining them."

To return to dream, "A Cure of Souls" has for its hero "the
pastor/of grief and dreams." Just as in the early "Homage," the
poet praises the person who lives "solitary in your empire of
magic, dreaming wideawake," so in "A Turn of the Head"
Emerson is heroic because he is "a good dreamer." Man in
"Shalom" speaks of "dreams/burnt in the bone" as "Starladen
Babylon/buzzes in his blood, an ancient pulse." In the 1964
collection, emphasis on dream as archetypal knowledge is
coupled with a somewhat new interest in rite and ritual.

Consonant with her professed admiration for Jungian thought,
she turns to the answer of ritual in one group of poems from *O
Taste and See*. "In Abeyance" deals with the essential respect for
man, god, and life inherent in the classic customs of anointing,
feasting, giving gifts, sacrificing. The deep contrast with today's
culture exists because "we are so many." And yet, even the
most desperate of modern men have "their days of grace, they/
halt, stretch, a vision/breaks in on the cramped grimace,/
inscape of transformation./Something sundered begins to knit./
By scene, by sentence, something is rendered/back into life, back

to the gods." In an earlier poem, "Beyond the End," Levertov
had implied that the search for rite, for pattern, was innate. She
described a crowd of shoppers:

> the girls crowding the stores, where light,
>   colour, solid dreams are—what gay
> desire! It's their festival,
>   ring game, wassail, mystery.

> *(Here and Now, 6)*

In another late poem, "The Novices," man and boy are
initiated into life by a process described as "rite." They have
only to realize that even a "feather of broken/oracle" is valuable.
"The Prayer" describes an experience that follows closely the
Jungian pattern of self-discovery—boredom, the new but fearful,
the daring to experience, and adjustment with its resulting expansion. As a result of the poet's prayer to Apollo—though, as
the poem implies, Apollo may not have been the god who
answered—she is filled with that which "burns and chills,
blackening/my heart with its soot,/flaring in laughter, stinging/
my feet into a dance." Her quest for experience has brought new
knowledge of self.

Bringing ritual—and the knowledge of and respect for other
men basic to its practices—into one's life is a way of maintaining
composure amid chaos. At times in Levertov's poetry it seems
that man can only gain by steeping himself in ritual.

The poet's use of the forms of psalm, prayer, and rune; her
reliance on incantation and refrain; her interest in death, water,
serpents, and various Earth Mother figures—each practice illustrates further her respect for man's basic responses. This is not
to say that Levertov makes use of traditional poetic symbols as
such; hers is not an allusive, erudite poetry. Her reference
pattern is more instinctive and feminine than it is "literary." The
Fisher King does not appear; instead, Xochipilli, Alpheus, the
forest bear, Ishtar, the Turtle Goddess, and the muse represent
some form of deity.

One of the most pervasive sets of images in Levertov's poetry
is that of seas, rivers, fountains, wells—all sources of nourishment and of life. "The Fountain" is a most poignant plea for
belief: "Don't say, don't say there is no water/to solace the dry-

ness at our hearts." In "The Well," the muse brings "life, spring water"; and her act is compared with that of Annie Sullivan, "she who/spelled the word 'water' into the palm/of Helen Keller, opening/the doors of the world."

Although Levertov has frequently written of archetypal images, she has seldom used specific myths. In the 1960 poem "Matins," however, the Conn-Edda symbols of iron ball and horse appear. In 1964 Levertov explained her rationale for this usage—that an allusion to myth is acceptable, she feels, so long as the myth is a personal one and not just a "trick." She chose this particular legend because she had dreamed that she had a part in it, and therefore she was personally identified with it.

> "It was my hope that the symbols, the images in themselves would carry what the story was saying. . . . I have made a great deal of use of dream material, and I have justified the use of apparently personal material to which one might say that the reader wouldn't have the clues, by hoping that such dream material as I have used would again speak for itself and have some correspondence with the dream material of others, enough to give it universality."[2]

The poem "Matins" is a full statement of many of her beliefs about dream and reality, or "the authentic" as she designates it in the poem. "Shadows of it/sweep past in dreams. . . . You/recognize it before you have time." The child of the poem has "clear sight" because "his black eyes hold his dreams"; his recognition—or anyone's—will be a surprising process, with "the known/appearing fully itself, and/more itself than one knew."

Recognition is, however, elusive. As in the Conn-Edda myth, man has little recourse but to break through appearances to the "true forms" beneath. In this conjunction, Levertov describes "the real" as "the new-laid/egg whose speckled shell/the poet fondles and must break/if he will be nourished."

As many lines in "Matins" suggest, no poet has been more concerned with the objective realities of life. Levertov realized early, however, that things are important chiefly for their personal value to the poet. The distinguishing characteristic of an object is its relevance to the observer. The scenery of "The Coming Fall," memorable as it is for its physical beauty, is more important for its power to evoke in the poet "a sense of the present/ . . . a wisdom,/a shiver, a delight/that what is passing/is here." Another glimpse of nature is meaningful as representing "an absolute patience."

In the last analysis, it is the recognition of one's own person that is most meaningful: "Not history, but our own histories,/a brutal dream drenched with our lives." In some respects, life exists as an extension of personality: inner experience determines the validity of the extraneous—the validity and the value. As one basic principle of artistic growth, Levertov has said, "The artist must/create himself or be born again."[3] Such creation, or re-creation, implies a thorough self-knowledge, a ready awareness. The mature poet, then, sees clearly enough to be afraid, yet is also confident of his power to meet and act against that fear. "September 1961," "Kingdoms of Heaven," "The Secret," "The Novel"—all reflect the surety that evolves from knowing what opposes one, and knowing too one's own power to meet that opposition: "to believe it's there/within you/though the key's missing/makes it enough."

II *Music as Theme, as Poem*

Not all of Levertov's beliefs have been expanded, of course. She has derived much of her personal and artistic confidence, I would surmise, from the primary tenets which have continued unchanged throughout her writing. Because one of her loves is certainly the poem, the constancy of her beliefs about poetry has undoubtedly given her stability in many ways.

For example, her definition of the poem and the poetic process does not change. Even though parts of the making of a poem must be inexplicable, she feels that critical direction is essential in nearly all phases of the process. She writes in a review of Louis Zukofsky's work: "And how much the many young poets who are living on a diet of public confession, made without care for craft, and therefore being only on the edge of the art of poetry, might learn from Zukofsky of 'That order that of itself can speak to all men.' "[4] Craftsman that she is, Levertov shares with Charles Olson his interest in the tension among the parts of the poem, the reciprocity among words, images, structure. Olson describes these interrelationships as a "field of force," a lateral, spatial congruence.[5] Levertov tends to modify that pattern, to see the poem as a whorl of particles formed around a central sound, a tone that influences pace, word choice, and spatial arrangement. She refers to this sound which is peculiar to each poem as the "horizon note."[6]

Pace, tempo, horizon note—musical terminology runs throughout Levertov's criticism and poetry. The use of words from the vocabularies of painting, sculpture, and music is not unusual; ironic though it is, few adequate critical terms exist for discussing poetry. Then, too, applying musical terms to poetry broadens the implications of the latter. When Levertov titles some poems "psalms" or "songs," the reader is alerted to the song-like qualities of those poems: rhythms, refrains, word patterns, sounds rather than literal meanings of words. With the poet's interest in musical forms has come an increasing use of musical patterns in the structure of her poems. Many are divided into distinguishable movements, differing in pace and tone; others are one-theme, one-note lyrics; some are intricate madrigals. Her first sequence of poems, for example, is titled "Notes of a Scale."

Levertov draws some critical terminology from painting and sculpture, but her primary interest lies in music. The personal reason for this affinity with music is that she studied ballet for years, both in England as a girl and in Mexico after her marriage. It is natural that she employ some terms from this field of formal training—just as T. S. Eliot drew on the idioms of philosophy and William Carlos Williams on those of medicine and science.

Poetically, she sees the dance as a means of total physical expression. In the shapes of the ballet figures, particularly in the leap, she finds a depiction of the harmony and exuberance possible in life. The concept of harmony itself implies balanced form as well as balanced tone, and reinforces again her purpose for writing: to reflect the natural accord she finds in existence. It is fitting, then, that images of dance represent this accord within her poems. Rain dances. The words of the sea are spoken in a "crash/and sighing dance." Movement of a New York winter night is "a dance to the compass points." The mystic poet-water-woman "goes dancing in the misty lit-up town"; and the cat sporting with a mouse is "an angel/dancing with his prey"—his dance, "a prayer!"

In contrast, most contemporary people in Levertov's poems sit, blunder, jostle: they are graceless, tired, apathetic, "mourning or ghostwalking only." That she equates the creative movement of dance with the creative process of art, or of living, comes as no surprise. Besides being archetypal, the theme has been constant throughout her own poetry. In *Here and Now*, people lack energy, zest, to live fully: they are not aware, they do not respond. In *With Eyes at the Back of Our Heads*, as the title suggests, Levertov decides that the root of this dullness lies in blindness. Maybe new means of perceiving would revivify life: "learn to see again," "Renew the power men had in Azerbaijan/to cast ethereal intensity in bronze." Power comes through new vision. The theme of seeing also dominates *O Taste and See*, but perception is expanded to a more inclusive emotional involvement. This sensory emphasis had been foreshadowed in *The Jacob's Ladder* when the sights in "Luxury" were recognized "without a direct look," "obliquely." In that same collection, "sight" was defined as a spiritual apperception, and the poet had come to see life "as more than a colloquy of objects."

Earlier poems too had indicated that sight was not the complete answer. In "Girlhood of Jane Harrison," Levertov pays tribute to the classic scholar by identifying her as the "dancer" whose movement breaks through darkness and shadows:

> The dance was a stamping in
>
> of autumn. A dance in the garden
> to welcome the fall . . .
>
> Multiplied,
>
> the dancer moved outward to all the
> promontories of shadow, the
>
> forest bays, the moon islands.
>
> (*Eyes*, 25)

And the equation of the cat's dance and prayer is further reflection on the *participation mystique* of primitive cultures: the dance then held the place of prayer today. This belief is illustrated most movingly in her poem "In Obedience," written in 1958, as a young daughter reacts to her father's approaching death:

> I dance
> for joy, only for joy
> while you lie dying, into whose eyes
> I looked seldom enough, all the years,
> seldom with candid love. Let my dance
> be mourning then,
> now that I love you too late.
>
> (*Overland,* 11)

Once man can see or move well, his responsibility is to act, either through further motion or through "construction." Levertov's use of this latter term implies that the art product is to be a tangible object. Already, however, there have been indications that the poem for Levertov is more than a "mass of crude substance." As she had written in "The Charge,"

> You must make, said music
>
> in its voices of metal and wood
> in its dancing diagrams, moving
> apart and together, along
> and over and under a line
> and speaking in one voice,
>
> make
>
> my image.
>
> (*Eyes,* 11)

No longer an object, "image" here relates to an evanescent impression, a sound. And although music has "dancing diagrams," its image is chiefly one of "voice." The poem "A Music" also couples the principles of movement and sound, as barges moving downstream create "melody," moving as they do "a little

> faster perhaps
> or is it
> slower?—a
> singing
> sung if it is sung
> quietly
>
> (*The Jacob's Ladder,* 43)

Movement here is equated with sound, set as it finally is amid the "scored crashing" and the "hum" of the river. In "The Tulips," Levertov also describes motion in terms of sound, as tulip petals "fall/with that sound one/listens for."

Indicative of her modification of terms, in later poems movement becomes subordinate to sound: dance is absorbed into the more general designation of "song," "music," as are its terms. Whereas in early work, music served as background for the experience of the poem, in recent poems, sounds become the primary impression. "Six Variations," one of Levertov's longer, sequential poems, works explicitly with the sounds of life. The central sound is that of Basket, Gertrude Stein's dog, drinking.

> Shlup, shlup, the dog
> as it laps up
> water
> makes intelligent
> music, resting
> now and then to
> take breath in irregular
> measure.

The fact that this most natural of sounds—unpatterned and "irregular"—creates "intelligent music" is the key to the theme of the poem. For in contrast to the dog's music come ineffective, often destructive words. For example, Stanza IV presents an anguished conversation, "when your answers/come/slowly, dragging/their feet:

> a lagging leaden pace,
> a short sullen line,
> measure
> of heavy heart and
> cold eye.

Although Stanza V brings contrasting jubilance, an indiscriminate reaction by "blind love," "nature," "the quick of the sun," Stanza VI returns with a culminating metaphor, uniting the tortured words and that most natural of sounds, Basket's drinking:

> Lap up the vowels
> of sorrow,
>   transparent, cold
> water-darkness welling
> up from the white sand . . .

Dignity lies in the "speech" of Basket, in the unstudied dance of the gnats, in old man Volpe's almost inarticulate but genuine communication (as he "made up what words he didn't know").

Although the relationship between theme and the techniques used to create it will be discussed more thoroughly in Chapter IV, a word about the poet's basic approach here is, I feel, appropriate—particularly since one theme in "Six Variations" is technique. Line arrangement is one of the most effective devices in this particular poem. The length of the line indicates consistent tempo as well as change within that tempo. Stanza V, the jubilant passage, moves in long, more nearly run-on lines[7] comprised of principal words—nouns, adjectives—united by the dominant sound of a sibilant (*s, c*):

> the fluted
> cylinder of a new ashcan a dazzling silver,
> the smooth flesh of screaming children a quietness, it is all
> a jubilance

Mournful Stanza IV, in contrast, moves in lines of three to five syllables, each short word emphasized so that each line moves slowly:

> When I can't
> strike one spark from you,
> when you don't
> look me in the eye . . .

(The Jacob's Ladder, 16-18)

Short words and short lines dominate the poem, but there are important changes in movement. After all, Levertov is working with "variations."

Indentation of lines, a device used frequently in her early poetry, has almost disappeared in the poems of the 1960's. When she does use what E. E. Cummings called "vertical space," the practice is effective. In "Six Variations," only two lines are indented: "slowly, dragging" in Stanza IV and "transparent cold" in VI. Both lines are key "asides" in descriptive passages, serving to create a rhythmic pause as well as to intensify meaning.

Levertov uses the same principles of arrangement in one of her best late poems, "Claritas." Here the song of the "All-Day Bird, the artist" is the controlling metaphor. The action of the poem is concerned with the bird's attempts to sing and his prayer for the perfect song. The poem culminates in a stanza re-creating the sparrow's song, read by Levertov with noticeable modulation in pitch, to duplicate the actual bird song. The entire poem is a wonderfully controlled piece of movement, with a consistent tone and pace in each stanza, even that of the bird's song. The short lines are made up of words which are correspondingly short and primary. Again, only two lines are indented, those of single words: *prays* and *light*. Both words are important to the theme of the poem—the clarity the devout bird-artist achieves

> striving
> in hope and
> good faith to make his notes
> ever more precise, closer
> to what he knows.
>
> (*O Taste*, 35)

"What he knows" is reverence for a greater power, and perfection for his song. In that lies "claritas"—not in an abstraction but in a sound.

As these poems and many others from her work show, song is a means of communicating honestly. Music, then, becomes a counterpart of the warm silence Levertov finds so expressive. Not only does nature "sing" (its mountains, woods, rivers, birds); music rises as well from men who have well-being, integrity, promise. In fact, any man who has lived is said to have had a music. In "The Dead" Levertov describes the process of dying as "a music, however harsh, that held us/however loosely, had stopped."

Men have a music, but the creation of song appears to be the duty of the poet. The artist in "Claritas" forms song. Walking through her notebooks, Levertov experiences both dance ("the flame-tango,/the smoke-gavotte") and song. Her poet *personae,* Melody Grundy and the "turbulent moon-ridden girl," both know "strange songs." As in "Claritas," the equation of the poet and the religious seer becomes stronger through the relation of both to the song and the song-making process. In "Earth Psalm," mortal man has the power to laugh, to speak, and most important, like Orpheus, to make "a music" which can turn the heads of all beasts. Music is associated with the religious impulse not only in this psalm and in the powerful "Psalm Praising the Hair of Man's Body," but in "Three Meditations" in which the battlefield of the world stirs with "unheard litanies, sounds of piercing green"; and in "The Fountain" where the life-giving water possesses "its quiet song and strange power."

Song, however, need not always be created. It exists in nature, and can be enjoyed there by any listener. In "Who Is at My Window," Levertov distinguishes between "the old song" which is about "fear, about/tomorrow and next year" and the meaningful song, about the present. This song is found again in "Another Spring," the essence of which is "music to sing to," and in several of the love poems, "Love Song" and "Song for a Dark Voice."

As this brief survey has attempted to show, the themes of Levertov's poetry could be said to stem from her concern with man's total being—his intellectual and mystical experiences; his physical relationships; his attempts to communicate—either through music, or silence, or words. Especially in recent poems, she appears to be asking what is the role of the humane man, of the religious man, of the poet, but to be aware of life and to share that awareness? As she writes in the last part of "Three Meditations": the conflicts of life are all, finally, directed toward

> bringing the poet
> back to song
> as before
>
> to sing of death
> as before
> and life, while he
> has it, energy
>
> being in him a singing,
> a beating of gongs, efficacious
> to drive away devils . . .
>
> to be
> what he is
> being his virtue
>
> filling his whole space
> so no devil
> may enter.

CHAPTER *4*

'The Sound of Direction'

I *The Rationale of Sound*

LEVERTOV'S increased use of sounds as subject matter for her poetry is only one phase of a general interest which has given her recent work an important technical focus. In fact, this emphasis may well be the means for her artistic development. She is working intensely with the oral impression of the poem, its sound as created from line and stanza arrangement, patterns of vowel and consonant (and entire word) repetition, onomatopoetic effects, and many other poetic devices.

In her discussion of harmony, horizon note, pace, and rest, she uses the terms literally because, in her rationale for poetry, the poem is an oral art form. As she explained in a 1964 interview, "sounds can carry the emotion of the poem. . . .

> I'm increasingly uninterested in what Pound has called phanopoeia, as such—the poetry of the visual image. I think the visual image is terribly important, but it must be accompanied by the melopoeia, and melopoeia of a distinctly expressive kind, not just the musical over and aboveness that Pound speaks of in his definition in *How to Read*. Something closer to onomatopoeia, actually. . . .
>
> I would like to say that one of the most important things for me . . . is the way the form arises from the sound of the words. It's not a matter of merely connotative precision. I mean that every time there is a choice (and there is a constant choice, as a matter of fact) of words meaning the same thing, one must be able to choose the one that corresponds in sound the most closely to the thing being spoken of. It's that thing Pound speaks of, quoting Dante, about words being buttery or shaggy. If one is speaking of something fine, thin, and sharp, one has to choose the words that have the finest, thinnest, lightest, sharpest sound, and not words that have round, dark, warm, thick sounds.[1]

This particular belief explains her interest in the critical writings of Edith Sitwell, one of the few contemporary poets to explain her diction in terms of sounds. It may also explain the difficulty readers have in placing Levertov; emphasis on sound *per se* has been rare in modern work, except for that of Hilda Doolittle and Wallace Stevens. Critics may need to begin thinking of Levertov as one of the *meistersingers* of contemporary poetry.

I do not mean to infer that Levertov writes songs. These are poems, but poems in which patterns of sounds work subtly into the total effect—so subtly that many readers are not aware of them. But again and again during that second stage of poetic appreciation, when the warming sense of rightness gives way to curiosity about that rightness, the reader sees that a complex sound pattern lies at the heart of the poem's impression. Levertov's concern for the oral effect, however, is always proportionate: sound remains one component of the whole poem, but an increasingly important one. Her recent advice to a reader is that he "take time to read the poems aloud, or at least to *sound them out.*"[2] And in a 1963 review, she coins a term for the organization of some modern poems, "harmonic." Far different from standard linear form, harmonic form as she sees it

> is composed—as music may be out of a certain set of tones—from a relatively small number of key words which are used over and over, not in idle repetition but in a progression of phrases which take resonance and increased meaning from one another, and which, without mounting to a bombastic crescendo . . . have a parallel in the way a musical theme can be taken up by more and more instruments as its variations develop. Organic concord such as this is as different as possible from the dogged, pre-arranged insistence of prescribed forms like the villanelle.[3]

Such consideration of the sound of a poem was nearly synonymous with the word *poetry* until this century, when the reaction to basic artistic "traditions" brought much poetry away from "melody." An erroneous reading of the doctrines of Ezra Pound and William Carlos Williams led many writers into believing that prose was to be the language of poetry. What Pound and Williams were advocating with their talk of "actual speech" and "the colloquial" was, however, a return to some contemporary language rhythms, a technique as traditional as any known. Because of this misunderstanding, however, some modern poetry sounds like dulled, vapid conversation. In contrast to this effect, much of Levertov's work contains a skillfully wrought word music.

As her comments show, she realized that the emphasis on "natural speech" was an oversimplification. Then, too, she had within her reading (and hearing) experience many poets like Keats and Tennyson, for whom sound was central to poetry. As a result, she concluded that the words of common speech may in essence be the same as those of poetry, but that they are used differently. Poetry is more succinct than everyday speech, it is more often figurative; the root of the difference, however, probably lies in the movement of the words. As Levertov wrote, it is more "a question of rhythm and pace than of diction."[4]

Her poems "Leaving Forever" and "The Fountain" are good examples of contrasting effects when diction is similar but pace varies. In both poems assonance and even word repetition provide the basis for tonal pattern.

LEAVING FOREVER

He says the waves in the ship's wake
are like stones rolling away.
I don't see it that way.
But I see the mountain turning,
turning away its face as the ship
takes us away.

(*O Taste*, 25)

THE FOUNTAIN

Don't say, don't say there is no water
to solace the dryness at our hearts.
I have seen
the fountain springing out of the rock wall
and you drinking there. And I too
before your eyes

found footholds and climbed
to drink the cool water . . .

(*The Jacob's Ladder*, 55)

So far as diction goes, the words in both poems are simple, direct, and short. Both vocabularies draw from "actual speech" in that the poet as *persona* speaks throughout and, in one, uses indirect quotation. It should be noticed that there are words in "The Fountain" which might be unnatural in common conversation—*solace, The woman of that place, scalloped.* The words are suitable to this poem, however, partly because of the projected character of the *persona* (see pp. 97ff.) and partly because of the pace of the poem.

Despite many similarities between the poems, "The Fountain" is a stronger poem—and the difference in degree of success can be attributed at least partly to the difference in rhythm. The movement of "Leaving Forever" is rough because lines 2, 3, and 4 are end-stopped. Movement resumes awkwardly with each new line, creating a halting progression which is intensified by the line-end assonance of *wake, away, way,* and *away.* In contrast, "The Fountain" moves urgently in active, continuing sentences. The poem begins in a rush of emotion, initial momentum carrying through subsequent sentences. It moves by sentence rather than by line, although line divisions are valid indicators of both content and rhythm. Part of the immediacy of this poem comes from the use of *and* to relate phrases as well as lines.

Creating appropriate rhythms is one of the poet's most difficult tasks, particularly in the organic concept of poetry which Levertov professes. She considers each poem autonomous, its parts of necessity free from prescribed order so that they may fit each poem. Instead of placing a constant number of accents in each line, she tries to achieve a "rhythmic norm" for each poem, a pace which dictates word arrangement and, to some extent, word choice. There must inevitably be interaction between content and movement, as she explains: "This sense of the beat or pulse underlying the whole interacts with the nuances or forces of feeling which determine the emphasis on one word or another, and decides to a great extent what belongs in a given line."[5]

Essentially, this is the quantitative approach to prosody, similar to that used in Greek verse. Rhythm is based on the duration of syllables as they are pronounced—an entirely oral standard. The Gregorian chant makes use of similar principles: words determine rhythm, but accordingly, too, words are chosen to meet the requirements of the total poem—both thematic and prosodic. In Levertov's best poetry, rhythm cannot be separated from diction. There is only a definite and consistent movement. As we have seen, she attributes this movement to the presence of a "horizon note" peculiar to each poem. Like its counterpart in music, this sound-pace dominates the poem despite variant passages. The horizon note is the basis for the "rhythmic norm" which can pervade not only a single poem but also groups of poems. She has pointed out, for example, that her poems "Song for Ishtar," "The Elves," and "The Ache of Marriage" are a rhythmic unit, although not seemingly a thematic one.

Such rhythmic interrelation suggests that one person's poetry may have as characteristic a movement as it does theme, imagery, or vocabulary. Such is the case with Levertov's work, it seems to me. The usual movement of her poetry is stately and slow, but it can rise to impassioned abruptness. Even her lighter poems tend to move dramatically, being filled with unexpected pauses, paradoxes, and careful changes in tempo. The near-sonority of much of her poetry results from a preponderance of long, dark vowels arranged so that each receives full time value. One notices the similarity of what the poet would call "textures" in the following excerpts from poems about very different themes:

> Death in the grassblade
> a dull
> substance, heading blindly
> for the bone
>
> ("Three Meditations," *The Jacob's Ladder,* 30)

> In the green Alameda, near the fountains,
> an old man, hands
> clasped behind his shabby back
> shuffles from rose to rose, stopping
> to ponder and inhale
>
> ("The Rose," *Ibid.,* 27)

> With a mirror
> I could see the sky.
>
> With two mirrors or three
> justly placed, I could see
> the sun bowing to the evening chimneys.
>
> ("The Room," *Eyes,* 28)

I have heard it said,
and by a wise man,
that you are not one who comes and goes

but having chosen
you remain in your human house

                    ("To the Muse," *O Taste*, 25)

The strikingly similar movement of these random selections
(published from 1959 to 1964, in three different collections) can
be attributed in part to several characteristic practices. One is
Levertov's fondness for long or long-sounding vowels. Often,
length of vowel is increased because it is followed by a stop:
punctuation, line ending, or combinations of consonants which
are difficult to pronounce (the *-th* in *Death*, the *-stly* in *justly*,
the *-sped* in *clasped*). The fact that Levertov uses many short
lines and monosyllabic words (or words which by their derivation fall into separate syllables as does *grassblade*) also slows
movement.

One chief difference between organic and traditional poetry
is that single words become more important in the first mode of
composition. Poets working in traditional rhyme patterns must
compose in phrases or, better, in sentences so that meaning is
clear in spite of adherence to pre-established forms. By being
free to concentrate on the individual word, the poet using an
organic mode can be more exacting—and presumably, more
accurate—in his expression.

This emphasis on the single word should make possible a more
purposeful work of art by giving the poet more control over
what happens in the poem and forcing him to scrutinize, to
weigh, not only each word but also each syllable. The use of
single words comes to be of great technical importance, for
characteristic effects can grow only from characteristic word
usage. As might be supposed, analyses of Levertov's poetry show
that she has developed such a body of verbal devices.

The technique in "The Fountain" is a good illustration of
characteristic use. Monosyllables dominate the poem, two of
them—*there* and *rock*—emphasized through repetition. Other
key words are equally simple and direct—*water, fountain, dryness, refreshed*. Perhaps because of the innately slow pace of a
line of short words, alliteration becomes very prominent. Here

the *r* and *w* patterns work amid the contrasting sibilants, *f* and *s* —all tending to maintain the intense pace. Primary justification for the intermediate third sentence ("The woman of that place . . . refreshed") is the effective sonority of the open *w* sound pattern. Again, vowels tend throughout to be long or nearly long, as in "scalloped green and gray stones."

The test of the success of any poetic device must be its relation to the poem as a whole. Here theme, movement, and tonal pattern are compatible. "The Fountain" is far from optimistic cajolery, although the tone is hopeful. It is a poem of awareness, awareness that few people see or believe in the "fountain." The poet-speaker is combating what seems to be an omnipresent view, that there *is* no water. Even those who have found it in the past have forgotten; so she reminds them with a controlled yet desperate plea. Because of content, the poem demands the emphasis, the pause, that each word receives.

Although the verbal control in a poem like this should be clearly impressive, some readers feel that "free verse" is easy to write. In the following statement, Levertov describes the difficulties of leaving traditional rhyme patterns for verbal devices used organically. She discusses "rhythm" as "the whole metrical structure" of a poem: "The fact that there is no predetermined rhyme scheme by no means indicates that rhyme is to be discarded. Rhyme, chime, echo, repetition, can be of supreme importance in arriving at the just form of an experience. Not only do they serve to knit together its elements, but they are frequently the very means, the sole means, by which the density of texture and the quality of repetition within experience can be transmuted into language."[6]

"Rhyme, chime, echo, repetition"—by avoiding the words usually associated with verbal technique (assonance, alliteration, onomatopoeia, etc.), Levertov indicates her views. Although she uses all these traditional word devices, it is the larger pattern of word effects that is her primary interest. The fact that *found footholds* is an alliterative phrase is negligible; the fact that it is a key thematic phrase, linked to the rest of "The Fountain" through the sibilant sound pattern, is important. Levertov does not avoid alliteration or assonance, but she does avoid building poems around such devices.

Of all single verbal devices in Levertov's work, assonance

proves to be the most effective, perhaps because it is the most viable. In some poems it is used only to set the initial mood; in others it permeates the entire poem. These lines from "Turning" illustrate the merging of a single vowel sound (the long *a*) into a more open pattern to unite later sections of the work:

> The shifting, the shaded
> change of pleasure
>
> Soft warm ashes in place of fire
> out, irremediably
>
> and a door blown open . . .
>
> *(Overland,* 8)

The last line quoted is especially characteristic of the poet's use of assonance: the patterned vowels come within major thematic words so that assonance is consequently unobtrusive. Because the vowels emphasized often fall in basic words (*someone, line, two*), sound patterns are integral to the poem, not ornamental.

The beginning quatrain of "The Secret" moves effortlessly and yet introduces *life* and *line,* key words for the subsequent verbal pattern:

> Two girls discover
> the secret of life
> in a sudden line of
> poetry.

So natural sounding is this opening that its verbal patterns merit no special attention. A few verses later, however, the poem builds to a climactic passage of dense vowel repetition.

> I love them
> for finding what
> I can't find,
>
> and for loving me
> for the line I wrote,
> and for forgetting it
> so that
>
> a thousand times, till death
> finds them, they may
> discover it again, in other
> lines . . .
>
> *(O Taste,* 21)

"The Secret" illustrates Levertov's use of sustained assonance, a technique she makes even more effective by staying within several major sounds, here, long *i* and short *o*. In this poem, Levertov is working with a concept she terms the *echo word*, a more limited kind of assonance (see p. 88). The words *find, line,* and *time* do not rhyme; but their impressions are like enough to create a semblance of irregular internal rhyme. The same is true of *for;* its repetition suggests an intentional pattern which culminates, perhaps ironically, in the composite word, *forgetting.*

Although the concept of echo word is very important in Levertov's poetry, it may well be that her use of such a close sound pattern in "The Secret" is responsible for this poem's ultimate weakness, at least when compared with "Another Spring":

> In the gold mouth of a flower
> the black smell of spring earth.
> No more skulls on our desks
>
> but the pervasive
> testing of death—as if we had need
> of new ways of dying? No,
>
> we have no need
> of new ways of dying.
> Death in us goes on
>
> testing the wild
> chance of living
> as Adam chanced it.
>
> Golden-mouth, the tilted smile
> of the moon westering
> is at the black window, . . .

Here, elements of several word patterns in the opening stanzas coalesce in verses four and five, the physical, structural, and thematic center of the poem. The dominant vowel sound (in *desk-test-Death-west*) builds to the climactic "Death in us goes on/testing," a reversal of the earlier "testing of death," and is then subdued in "westering" which leads to the final, assured statement, despite the reference to the death's-head figure, Calavera. The repetition of *chance* in the somewhat cacophonic phrase "the wild chance of living/as Adam chanced it" contrasts with the earlier sonorous repetition of "as if we had need/of new ways of dying?" This variation in both movement and sound parallels the content of the poem.

In "Another Spring," as in other of her best poems, figurative language is so integral a part of the poem that it is included in any verbal pattern. In the sensual figure of the gold-mouthed flower begins the repetition of *l*'s. She uses the *l* sound in the words *black, smell,* and *skulls;* but the inclusion of the harsh *k* sound foreshadows the change in mood. The *k* then links *skulls* with *desks,* and the dominant pattern of assonance is launched.

After the climactic fourth stanza, the pacific *m-l* sound is re-asserted as if reflecting the poet's affirmation of life, indicated also in the title. *Westering* bridges the central assonance and the later, its open *w* lending softness to both patterns. In *Golden-mouth, tilted smile, moon westering,* and *black window,* the tone of the closing three stanzas is introduced:

> Calavera of Spring.
> Do you mistake me?
> I am speaking of living,
>
> of moving from one moment into
> the next, and into the
> one after, breathing
>
> death in the spring air, knowing
> air also means
> music to sing to.
>
> (*O Taste,* 16-17)

Characteristically, too, the *m*'s, *n*'s, *s*'s, and *l*'s of this allitera-tive pattern fall within the principal words of the poem—*golden, moon, living, moving, moment, music, spring,* and *sing.* So basic are these words to the pervasive themes that sound patterns recur frequently. One should notice in this passage of apparent *g-s* domination, the number of labial and nasal tones:

> the shadows of September
> among the gold glint of the grass
>
> among shining
> willow leaves the small birds moving
>
> silent in the presence of a new season.
> ("The Coming Fall," *O Taste,* 38)

The frequency of these continuants is explained partly by the fact that the poet uses many *-ly* and *-ing* endings. Unlike some contemporary poets, she does not avoid modifiers, if those modifiers are necessary to her desired effect. For example, "About Marriage" illustrates the degree of difference possible between sections of "plain speaking" and description. The poem opens with the poet's plea,

> Don't lock me in wedlock, I want
> marriage, an
> encounter—
>
> I told you about the
> green light of
> May

Moving from "the green light of May" Levertov depicts a late spring afternoon when the poet encountered three birds and their mates. The adjectives used to describe the birds create a rhythm suggestive of the freedom demanded initially:

> the azalea-breasted with round poll, dark,
> the brindled, merry, mousegliding one,
> and the smallest, golden as gorse and wearing
> a black Venetian mask.

Although the passages are thematically much different, they are related through similar sounds, again chiefly the continuants *l* and *m*. In the concluding stanzas Levertov resumes her statement of desire, a descriptive statement strangely devoid of modifiers except for the adjectives *green* and *airy*, words which have thematic importance as well as descriptive:

> It's not
> irrelevant:
> I would be
> met
>
> and meet you
> so,
> in a green
>
> airy space, not
> locked in.
>
> (*O Taste,* 68-69)

The recurring sound patterns so evident in Levertov's work can also be explained partially by her use of favorite words, many of which contain *l, m,* or *n,* and *s* sounds: *silence, rippling, alone, black, nature,*[7] *love, mountain, smoke, shine, noon, stone, dance, endlessly, fountain, leaves, still, moon, dreams, silver, flower, hill, long, flame, wind, fall, closed, burn, song, silk, chill, flesh, light, gold, bone, land,* and *lake.* It is interesting that such a random list reflects her pervasive use of nature and its images within her poetry. No matter how well-liked individual words are, of course, they cannot be used unless they fit the needs of the poem to be written. As a rule, various types of poems require various vocabularies: narratives usually contain many nouns and verbs; personal lyrics, abstractions; descriptions, modifying words. That poems are of the same type in no way implies a uniform effect, however. As two scenic descriptions—"One A.M." and "Scenes from the Life of the Peppertrees"—show, Levertov creates two very much different poems from similar sound patterns, both heavy with assonance and alliteration.

ONE A.M.

The kitchen patio in snowy
moonlight.   That
snowsilence, that
abandon to stillness.
The sawhorse, the concrete
washtub, snowblue. The washline
bowed under its snowfur!
Moon has silenced
the crickets, the summer frogs
hold their breath.
Summer night, summer night, standing
one-legged, a crane
in the snowmarsh, staring
at snowmoon!

(*Overland,* 22)

Few poems present such unity of theme and sound. The major impression of the summer night—moonlit silence—is created through repetition of phrase as well as through key words within the description (*snow* used as prefix). The sounds of the poem, particularly the long vowels, build toward the concluding metaphor, summer night being "a crane/in the snowmarsh," serving as the climax for the description as well.

Although Levertov has achieved this masterful single tone, some readers may prefer the contrasting sounds of the Pepper-tree poem. In it the basic *l, m, n,* and *s* alliteration is accented with the plosives *p, t,* and *c* (*k*); part of the contrast is inherent in the subject matter of cats and trees:

> . . . Branch above branch, an air
> of lightness; of shadows
> scattered lightly.
>
> > A cat
> closes upon its shadow.
> Up and up goes the sun,
> sure of everything.
> > The peppertrees
> > shiver a little.
>
> Robust
> and soot-black, the cat
> leaps to a low branch. Leaves
> close about him.
>
> > > (*Overland,* 18)

As these poems show, alliteration can be a most effective verbal device. It can also be misused very easily because it is simple to attempt. Ostensibly, alliteration is the repetition of initial consonants; actually, good alliteration occurs only when the words so united through consonants have other bases for union—similar internal vowel sounds, corresponding positions, or parallel contrasts within the words themselves.

Like alliteration in that they too are considered "elementary" by some contemporary poets, consonance and onomatopoeia seem fresh as Levertov uses them. Consonance, the shifting of vowels within alliteration, appears in her work only rarely, and then amid other verbal devices. In the last stanza of "Resting Figure," it adds needed contrast to internal rhyme:

> strength and despair
> quiet there in the bed,
> the line of his limbs
> half-shown, as under stone
> or bronze folds.
>
> > > (*The Jacob's Ladder,* 36)

Onomatopoeia is a key technique for the poet, believing as she does that the poem is to be heard. Throughout her poems, experimentation with this device has been fruitful. She uses it equally well for a single effect or as the basis for entire poems. "Night on Hatchet Cove" shows her skill in contrasting sounds, a more difficult use of onomatopoeia than is a single uniform presentation. The first section of this poem is filled with words which are in themselves onomatopoetic: *whines, clacks, crackle, seething*. The second part, however, re-creates a deep quiet as accurately as the first has re-created sounds, using no words which in themselves are onomatopoetic.

The full effect of "Night on Hatchet Cove" results not merely from its representation of sounds; it stems in large part from the movement of the poem:

> The screendoor whines, clacks
> shut.   My thoughts crackle
> with seaweed-seething diminishing
> flickers of phosophorus.   Gulp
> of a frog, plash
> of herring leaping;
>   interval;
> squawk of a gull disturbed, a splashing;
> pause
> while silence poises for the breaking
> bark of a seal: but silence.
>   Then
> only your breathing. I'll
> be quiet too.   Out
> stove, out lamp, let
> night cut the question with profound
> unanswer, sustained
> echo of our unknowing.

> *(The Jacob's Ladder*, 13)

The most obvious use of arrangement in this poem is the isolation of *interval, pause,* and *Then,* with the word *pause* less emphasized in its position at the left margin. Levertov also uses vertical space to indicate stops after *shut* and before *Gulp.* This is the obvious visual pattern, but less noticeably effective is the arrangement of single words. A screen door, for example, does "whine" and then "clack shut," the abruptness of *clacks* accented by the line ending.

"Night on Hatchet Cove" provides a good illustration of Levertov's use of line arrangement and typography as guides to reading. All prescriptions of set form give way before her intention to help the reader-listener hear the poem as it was written to be heard. Line length and spacing are determined by the poem's rhythmic requirements, as are stanza divisions. Punctuation and indentation also serve primarily as guides to the poem's movement. However, although arrangement is a means to interpretation, most of the poems are remarkably conventional in appearance: they have stable margins, reasonably constant line length, and predictable punctuation. Any deviation from the norm in her poetry therefore is dramatic, and the reader accepts the "stage direction" because it is rare.

Proof of Levertov's increasing skill with words is the fact that in her late poems she seldom resorts to any variation in spacing and indentation. She achieves even line pace through words themselves instead of through arrangement. In short, visual effects—though they do exist—are subordinate to oral ones. This subordination is true also of "Night on Hatchet Cove." Although its typography is interesting and its onomatopoeia striking, the poem gains much of its effect from its total word pattern. I have referred to *seething* as an onomatopoetic word; actually the phrase in which it appears—"seaweed-seething diminishing flicker of phosphorus"—suggests the movement described. Levertov uses a similar technique in these phrases: "Gulp/of a frog, plash/of herring leaping." No adjectives or polysyllabic words are found; there are just plosive consonants, short words, and abrupt line endings. The last stanza carries this practice even further in its concluding long sentence ("profound/unanswer, sustained/echo of our unknowing"), a sentence not rhythmically unlike the long breath of the sleeping man.

Standard poetic devices—arrangement, assonance, alliteration, onomatopoeia—but the distinguishing quality about Levertov's use of them is that they seldom appear to be superimposed on a poem. We feel that the poem begins, and that *then* the poet draws from techniques germane to that beginning. "One A.M.," the title itself a statement of fact, opens with a second factual phrase: "The kitchen patio in snowy/moonlight." Though short, the opening phrase contains all major components of the poem—the long *o* sound as well as the dominant themes. A similar compatibility between opening tone and pervasive effect is evident in most of the poems.

Just as the opening of a poem is characteristic of that particular poem, so is Levertov's use of each verbal device. Her employment of alliteration does not bring to mind any general pattern; the repetition indicated may occur within one line or twenty. Assonance may grow from a series of words; it may also be built from the repetition of single words. Inventive use of existing devices leads eventually to the creation of techniques peculiarly her own. This is the case with the repeated single word which is often the basis for both assonance and theme.

II *The Echo Word*

Throughout Levertov's work, but increasingly in more recent poems, patterns of repeated single words appear. That she herself recognizes this practice as a definite technique is evident from her comment about the "echo word": "I particularly like the way repeated words weave strongly into the fabric, and the sense of word leading to echo word, not capriciously, but in a revelation of correspondences."[8] In this brief definition, Levertov shows that the echo-word pattern is to be flexible and subtly balanced. These repeated words, woven "strongly" together, provide "a revelation of correspondences." Although words are repeated, changing context provides variety. One value of this echo technique is that it permits the breadth of the word to be recognized; one finds a word in many contexts only to discover that it *is* appropriate throughout. In "Love Song," for example, the word *long* is the basis of the verbal pattern:

> Your beauty, which I lost sight of once
> for a long time, is long,
> not symmetrical, and wears
> the earth colors that make me see it.
>
> A long beauty, what is that?
> A song
> that can be sung over and over,
> long notes or long bones.
>
> Love is a landscape the long mountains
> define but don't
> shut off from the
> unseeable distance.

In fall, in fall,
your trees stretch
their long arms in sleeves
of earth-red and

sky-yellow. I take
long walks among them. The grapes
that need frost to ripen them

are amber and grow deep in the
hedge, half-concealed,
the way your beauty grows in long tendrils
half in darkness.

(*O Taste,* 6)

The central impression in the poem is that of "long beauty." The words *long* and *beauty* are coupled twice early in the poem, the second occurrence followed by a question heightening the strangeness of the phrase. The analogy (and rhyme) of "song/ that can be sung over and over" provides the relevant definition of long—lasting, timeless. The analogy is reinforced by the concluding phrase, "long notes or long bones." Incidental assonance of *over, notes,* and *bones* increases the sonority of this stanza; the word *long,* however, remains dominant.

Tempo changes in stanza three with the introduction of the formal metaphor, "Love is a landscape." Foreshadowed by "earth colors" in the opening stanza, this figure serves as the touchstone for the rest of the poem, although in her elaboration of it Levertov brings in the word *long* throughout—*long mountains, long arms, long walks.* These uses of *long* are like that which opened the poem, *long time;* they are natural uses, noticeable chiefly because of the central definition of *long beauty* in stanza two. Even in this comparatively simple usage, however, the tone of *long* is consistently pleasant. The poet is careful to point out that the *long mountains* fill a necessary role in defining the landscape: they do not obstruct. And the *long arms* of the lovers' trees are sleeved in warm *earth colors.*

Much of the effectiveness of "Love Song" comes from this variety in context for the echo word. Except for the second stanza, *long* appears casually, keyed to the pervasive tone of direct admission. The second stanza also maintains the pace of thoughtful statement; in it, however, Levertov uses the rhetoric of repetition to establish her theme. Without this early stanza of definition, the later recurrence of *long* would be less effective; without the simplicity of the closing lines, the opening of the poem might seem tedious.

"Love Song" is well named in that much of its beauty results from its sound, its tempo as well as assonance. Part of its movement is determined by the effects of single words; part, by the length of sentences; part, by line division. The rapid movement of the last stanza parallels that of the opening and the central section; the second stanza with its shorter phrases parallels the fifth. Although the second stanza is more important thematically, both furnish needed contrast to the rapid movement surrounding them.

Stanzas three, four, and five elaborate the figure of love as a landscape, with their descriptions of mountains, trees, walks, and grapes. Levertov reminds the reader of her theme, however, through her use of the personal pronouns which add immediacy and through the repetition of *long*. Her concluding simile returns the poem to its opening image: *long tendrils* relates to the love-landscape-grape figure and to that of *long beauty*. In the same way, *half in darkness* refers to both the half-concealed grapes and to the poet's initial oversight.

Effective as this poem is, several others in the 1964 collection show that the echo-word device can fail. Apparently some duration is necessary to achieve its best effect. In extremely short poems like "Leaving Forever" and "The Stonecarver's Poem," the verbal play seems merely clever ("smallest inviolate/stone violet"). Also in some earlier poems—"The Way Through," "The Dogwood," "The Springtime"—sequences of repetition are less striking than those in "Love Song" because they are short, confined to passages of only a few lines:

> Drown us, lose us,
> rain, let us loose, so
> to lose ourselves, to career
> up the plunge of the hill.
>
> ("The Way Through," *Overland,* 3)

It is interesting that until the 1964 collection, Levertov had experimented most frequently with this word repetition in the

1958 *Overland to the Islands,* where she used it to best effect in "Lonely Man."

Also in *Overland to the Islands* appears one of her first "songs," so titled, "A Song." This poem employs a refrain along with an echo-word pattern. Together with the 1959 "Obsessions" and its irregular end rhymes of *hands, land, return,* and *burned,* "A Song" leads to the fine later poems, "Song for a Dark Voice" and "Psalm Praising the Hair of Man's Body." The reason these latter poems are stronger, I think, is that they have a marked, continuing rhythm. "Psalm" contains three refrain stanzas to help establish the incantatory pace, but the beat of "Song for a Dark Voice" rises from accented first syllables in nearly every line.

Levertov's interest in sound as a basic element of the poem is evident in these poems; in the heavily alliterative "Lagoon" and "A Straw Swan under the Christmas Tree"; and in many late poems, in all of which words are eminently suitable to total effects.

Admittedly, this sometimes capricious, sometimes judicious experimentation with language is the work of all poets, but it is work rarely done with Levertov's dedication and skill. In the present visually-oriented culture, she re-emphasizes a poetic technique which is largely oral, convinced that the contemporary poem must recapture a music. She describes this emphasis on sounds as an *"extended onomatopoeia*—the sounds of the poem imitate, not the *sounds* of an experience, which may be and often is soundless, or to which sounds contribute only incidentally— but the *feel* of the experience, its texture, pace, and emotional tone."[9] And because there are so many kinds of experience, the poet must have at his command a wealth of words.

CHAPTER 5

'Wear Shoes That Fit'

I *Patterns of Organization*

The best work is made
from hard, strong materials,
    obstinately precise—
the line of the poem, onyx, steel.

It's not a question of
false constraints—but
    to move well and get somewhere
wear shoes that fit.

To hell with easy rhythms—
sloppy mules that anyone can
    kick off or
step into . . .
              ("Art," *Eyes,* 71)

O NE OF THE MOST CONTROVERSIAL areas of modern
poetic theory is form—stanza patterns, line length and division, the total shape of the poem being written. Since the
Imagists popularized "free verse" in the United States early in
the twentieth century, there have been no rules governing the
external form of the poem. "Form is never more than an extension of content,"[1] Robert Creeley writes; or, as Levertov has
emended it, "Form is never more than a revelation of content."[2]
Many contemporary poets feel that the only valid form is the
organic, an arrangement that grows from the entity of the poem
itself and complements the poem *per se* by expressing its individual characteristics. Emerson was one of the first poets to
describe organic form; but the creation of blank verse, of all so-
called rigid patterns—from the sonnet to the villanelle—was
originally one poet's attempt to find a form responsive to the
needs of his own writing.

Because the issue of form is so controversial, and because it is basic to any poet's work, I shall quote heavily from Levertov's comments on this subject, first made in 1962 and revised for publication in 1965:

> There are many poets who do not agree that in the best poetry "the sense dictates the rhythm." Their argument is that a form, a chosen, preconceived form, is a discipline to which they must submit their otherwise formless material, and that the stricter the discipline the more the material is purged of dross. I would not deny that many good poems have been written by poets who hold this belief; but I think this is rather in spite of, than because of it. When a poet is truly gifted, when his sense of language is original and he is indeed inspired, that is, when the breath of his content blows through him like the wind in a tree, then poetry overcomes, overrules, the limitations he has imposed on it. When a poet using preordained forms, however, is not thus seized and overruled, he is more likely to distort his material than is a poet working in organic forms; he is more likely, for obvious reasons, to pad out his lines; and the exigencies of rhymes that are bound to occur at strictly prescribed intervals have led many a poet into saying a great deal that he did not mean.
>
> .   .   .   .
>
> One definition—though a partial one—of organic poetry might be that it is a *method of apperception;* i.e. of recognizing what we perceive, and is based on an intuition of an order, a form beyond forms, in which forms partake, and of which man's creative works are analogies, resemblances, natural allegories. Such a poetry is exploratory.
>
> How does one go about such a poetry? I think it's like this: First there must be an experience, a sequence or constellation of perceptions of sufficient interest, felt by the poet intensely enough to demand of him their equivalence in words: he is *brought to speech*. Suppose there's the sight of the sky through a dusty window, birds and clouds and bits of paper flying through the sky, the sound of music from his radio, feelings of anger and love and amusement roused by a letter just received, the memory of some long ago thought or event associated with what's seen or heard or felt, and an idea, a concept, he has been pondering, each qualifying the other; together with what he knows about history; and what he has been dreaming—whether or not he remembers it—working in him. This is only a rough outline of a possible moment in a life. But the condition of being a poet is that periodically such a cross-section, or constellation, of

experiences (in which one or another element may predominate) demands, or wakes in him this demand, *the poem*. The beginning of the fulfillment of this demand is to contemplate, to meditate; words which connote a state in which the heat of feeling warms the intellect.

It is—and again the terminology, inevitably, is religious—an act of faith. The poet launches himself into the unknown—for the experience not fully known until it is manifested in the poem which reveals its form. . . . Certainly the process of choosing a structure and conforming honorably to its demands, though it is not without interest, is not, in my experience, comparable. The organic process, in which one doesn't know what is going to happen next, uses more of oneself, more areas of one's being are called into play. This partially answers one of the questions I have posited: why I believe this approach to poetry is of value. Because the more areas called into play in the poet, the more profound the source of image and symbol, the deeper the responses awakened in the reader. Deep calleth unto deep.

.   .   .   .

Scrupulously used by gifted artists, the organic way offers, I think, scarcely realized possibilities for the exploration of life, and a way of communication that we have scarcely begun to apprehend.[3]

Levertov's theory is, then, that each poem has a particular form, rhythm, identity of its own; that form is or should be organic because of the innate order in all parts of life; that the organic approach to poetry is a means of perceiving and/or exploring one's own experience and of reaching other men significantly. Technically, the rhythmic norm peculiar to each poem will determine the length and position of line and stanza; and balance, a sense of proportion, must ascertain the shape of the total poem.

Obviously, the concept of organic poetry is not a prescriptive one. In that lies its difficulty. There is no home base in the composition of an organic poem. The writer of sonnets could feel reasonably confident that his poem was acceptable if it had fourteen lines and one of several rhyme and rhythm patterns. The free-form poet has no exterior criteria; he has only his own sense of rightness. Because of the terrifically individual nature of such composition, many poets are uneasy about their own work, and that of others. But observation of any serious modern poetry shows a surprising degree of technical similarity among poems of a particular period. In other words, the poet tends to re-use techniques which work for him; consequently, it seems to be possible to isolate and study the poetic devices used within the work.

Regarding total structure in Levertov's work, one finds that she initially tended to write short depictions of single emotions, experiences, or ideas. There is one theme, and the structure—sometimes a paragraph organization, again groups of fairly regular tercets or quatrains—reflects its simplicity. For example, there is the paragraph organization as the basis of "Love Poem":

> Maybe I'm a "sick part of a
> sick thing"
> > maybe something
> has caught up with me
> certainly there is a
> mist between us
> > I can barely
> see you
> > but your hands
> are two animals that push the
> mist aside and touch me.
> > > *(Here and Now, 12)*

Characteristic of the short poems in the volume *Here and Now* (1957) is the use of indented lines to show breaks in thought. Line arrangement has replaced punctuation as a guide to reading, but we may question its effectiveness, particularly in lines three to five when the indentation progresses toward the left margin.* Later, she wrote much more consistently from a stable

---

* The use of line arrangement to indicate pause is, admittedly, a common device; but it is also a comparatively simple one, likely to be misused. Levertov uses it to good effect in "Merritt Parkway" and "The Hands." It is interesting that many poets initially use staggered margins, just as they often overpunctuate, or punctuate overemphatically, by using a great many dashes, exclamation points, italics, parentheses. For example, this atypical stanza from Levertov's "Beyond the End":

> It's energy: a spider's thread: not to
> "go on living" but to quicken, to activate: extend:
> > Some have it, they force it—
> with work or laughter or even
> > the act of buying, . . .
> > > *(Here and Now, 6)*

left margin, allowing the sound of the words rather than their placement to convey meaning.

The same kind of generalization might be made about stanza form. Many of her early poems are written in free-form paragraphs, strophes of irregular numbers of lines. Increasingly, her more recent poems fall into tercets or quatrains, though always of a flexible nature—lines may be dropped in one place and added in another, but the basis of stanza division remains clear. In 1963 Levertov explained that, in her poetry at that time, perceptions tended to come in units of "quite regular, pulse-like duration." She often experienced "clusters of realization" in triads or quatrains; therefore she arranged poems accordingly.[4] As if to illustrate her statement, fairly regular stanzas mark the poems published unchanged from first drafts—"Losing Track," "Love Song," "Song for Ishtar," and others.

The progression of idea within "Love Poem," characteristic also of Levertov's work, illustrates her early premise that "there are no miracles but facts." She begins with factual details listed objectively—here, with no transition between statements. The passage of detail builds to an inclusive phrase, usually either a figure of speech ("your hands are two animals") or a generalization. In "A Silence," for example, the description of a broken rose, martins, and a vase leads to the poet's statement of "meaning" drawn from those descriptions: "Silence/surrounds the facts. A language/still unspoken."

Many of the later poems are organized in this detail-statement format, with a noticeable turn at times toward a conclusion heavily weighted with meaning. This emphasis on a definite content has led some critics to accuse Levertov of writing "closed" poems—poems for which only one interpretation is possible. Modern taste seems to favor the "open" poem in which the impact is largely incitatory and the conclusion is suggestive rather than didactic. The poems "The Dead" (closed) and "The Bird" (open) illustrate these opposing kinds of final statement:

THE DEAD

Earnestly I looked
into their abandoned faces
at the moment of death and while
I bandaged their slack jaws and

straightened waxy unresistant limbs and plugged
the orifices with cotton
but like everyone else I learned
each time nothing new, only that
as it were, a music, however harsh, that held us
however loosely, had stopped, and left
a heavy thick silence in its place.

(*Eyes,* 33)

THE BIRD

That crazy bird
always laughing—
he sits on the wall they are building,
the wall
which will hide the horizon,
and laughs like mad every time
we open our mouths to say
I love you I hate you etc.
He came only since
the green rain came and
softened everything, making
mud of the cracked
selfrespecting earth and rotting
the red flowers from their stems. Yes,
the rain, the trucks full
of pink bricks, that crazy
eavesdropping bird, came
together and finished
the days of burning, and silence, and distance.

(*Here and Now,* 24)

The openness of "The Bird" is achieved primarily through ambiguity—the "green rain" that "softened everything" is powerful indeed, if *everything* includes the personal relationships which are the heart of the poem; the bird himself; and, most relevant to this discussion of endings, the three nouns which conclude the poem, *burning, silence,* and *distance.* These words and the poem itself are most meaningful taken in the context of other of her themes (see Chapter II). In contrast, "The Dead" has no implication; all is direct statement, even to the definition of death as "heavy thick silence," the impression which closes the poem. The distinction between "open" and "closed" endings may be quite fine; the question remains to be answered whether or not the firmer statement of the "closed" poem contradicts the possibility of art.

In the same rather amorphous category with this controversy is the charge that Levertov writes Imagist poems. Imagist—now a term of censure, or at least of nostalgia—is usually designated as a kind of short single-theme poem relying on visual impact for its effect. An Imagist poem, in regard to the open-closed ending issue, would be in that it generally presents the image and lets the reader form his own conclusions, as does Pound's "In a Station of the Metro" ("The apparition of these faces in the crowd;/Petals on a wet, black bough.") or Adelaide Crapsey's "Triad" ("These be/Three silent things:/The falling snow . . . the hour/Before the dawn . . . the mouth of one/Just dead."). The fact that the current definition has little relationship to the original concept of Imagism is, I suppose, immaterial. To use the present meaning of Imagism, however, is in some ways to answer the critics who are concerned about Levertov's "closed" endings, for most Imagist poems are open. Both critical terms can hardly apply simultaneously to Levertov's work.

Other, more relevant categories seem imperative. Granted that each poem is individual and granted that criticism demands terms with which to discuss art, the following loose structural divisions may be more appropriate than the other designations mentioned. One group within Levertov's poems might be those short poems using the "world observed" pattern. This kind of poetry presents an object or scene from the external world, re-creating it through accurate, observable detail.

> Two bean-fed boys set bottles on the wall
> yesterday, and shyed at them for a half-hour
>
> ("Broken Glass," *Overland*, 25)

or

> Martha, 5, scrawling a drawing, murmurs
> "These are two angels. These are two bombs
>
> ("The Lesson," *Overland*, 27)

The poet assumes objectivity; at least she herself is not a *persona* in the poem. The poem may end with either a summarizing abstraction or an open suggestive phrase.

Many of her early poems, including the famous "Merritt Parkway" and "One A.M.," fall into this category. With *The Jacob's Ladder* in 1961, however, a variation in this pattern occurs as Levertov uses contrast within the poem. This organization, evident in "The Jacob's Ladder," (see p. 30) "Partial Resemblance," and "Night on Hatchet Cove," permits her to deal with at least two elements rather than a single subject. She often uses juxtaposition within these poems.

I have commented elsewhere that any artist eventually works toward inclusion, toward interrelation of the fragments of his society into a whole—or at least toward an attempt at some hypothetical whole.[5] This movement is, I think, evident in Levertov's poems. She begins with the early, simple depictions of parts of her culture; but she soon moves to the milieu of those parts, to other associations, and finally to her own part in the experience. She attempts to reach this interrelation as most poets have—structurally, through such means as contrast or series; thematically, through the use of recurring images or symbols and metaphor; and esthetically, through her exploration of her involvement in the life she has previously only described. This latter change in approach is probably the most important single modification in the course of Levertov's work. It can be described partly as a shift from a third-person (observer) point of view, to a first-person narration. The difference is made clear in these two poems:

POEM FROM MANHATTAN

Green-spined
river-bounded
desired of summer storms

                              (city, act of joy
Spring evenings in sea-light
facades relax
steel and stone float among clouds

                              (city, act of power
And always nightfall flicks
fantasy on black air
        chips of light
                scattered
flashing

                          (city, act of energy . . .
                      (*Here and Now,* 31)

A LETTER TO WILLIAM KINTER OF MUHLENBERG

Zaddik, you showed me
the Stations of the Cross

and I saw
not what the almost abstract

titles held—world upon world—
but at least

a shadow of what
might be seen there if mind and heart

gave themselves to meditation, . . .

From the bus, Zaddik,
going home to New York,

I saw a new world
for a while—it was

the gold light on a rocky slope,
the road-constructors talking to each other,

bear-brown of winter woods, and later
lights of New Jersey factories and the vast

December moon. I saw
without words within me, saw

as if my eyes
had grown bigger and knew

how to look without
being told what it was they saw.

(*The Jacob's Ladder,* 44-45)

The scene is the New York area in both poems, but in "Poem from Manhattan" the poet focuses on the generalized visual details of the city. She speaks of "Spring evenings" rather than any one evening; of "littered avenues" instead of a specific place. These details give rise to her also general phrases of praise ("city, act of power"). In "A Letter," the poet's reaction to the city is the center of the poem, with the factual detail used to emphasize the poet's new-found ability to see. A key word opens the poem. In Hasidic thought, "Zaddik" signifies the helper who leads man until man can go on alone. He ministers to body and soul, for both are interrelated. The theme of the poem is, certainly, the experience of the poet who has been so aided, an experience beginning in physical awareness but signifying much more. First-person perspective, in addition to adding immediacy and vividness to "A Letter," also makes possible its effective natural phrasing.

As a rule, one of the strengths of first-person point of view is its viability. After the poet announces to his reader that he is writing of himself, he is free to include all kinds of associations, digressions, memories. The fabric of meaning grows wider. The advantages are apparent: a means of using a natural diction and of capturing fresh reactions and subjects. The danger is that the poem will become too discursive or esoteric in its intimacy. As Levertov warns, the use of "I" in a poem is "valid when actually operative, invalid when what is really interesting is not *who* perceives, but what is perceived; i.e., when the 'I' is contemplative let us have the results of contemplation without the prefatory 'I sit here contemplating.' "[6]

It is interesting to me that there are very few first-person poems in *Here and Now,* but those few—"The Rights," "The Flight," "The Third Dimension"—are the best poems of the collection. This correlation holds true throughout Levertov's work (I think especially of "In Obedience" from *Overland to the Islands* and of "Pleasures," "A Letter," and "To the Snake" from *With Eyes at the Back of Our Heads*). By the time of *The Jacob's Ladder,* Levertov was framing many of the experiences in the first-person narrative. The strongest of the earlier poems— "A Letter to William Kinter," "Clouds," "From the Roof," "A Solitude," "In Memory of Boris Pasternak"—open with the poet's account of her experience, as in the Pasternak poem:

> That day before he died, a burnet moth
> come to town perhaps on a load of greens,
> took me a half-hour out of my way, or what
> I'd thought was my way . . .

Or, from "A Solitude":

> A blind man. I stare at him
> ashamed, shameless. Or does he know it?
> No, he is in a great solitude.

Then the poet moves into a personal reaction to her experience, almost a re-creation of the thought process. Often, subconscious or dream elements are brought in—one part of the total response available to a person. Frequently the poem ends very far from the point of its ostensible beginning. The Pasternak poem closes,

> I remember
> a dream two nights ago: the voice,
> "the artist must
> create himself or be born again."
>
> (*The Jacob's Ladder*, 32-33)

and "A Solitude," still apparently close to the experience but moving also into man's character,

> and now he says he can find his way. He knows
> where he is going, it is nowhere, it is filled
> with presences. He says, *I am*.
>
> (*The Jacob's Ladder*, 68-70)

This progression from third person point of view to first is logical for Levertov who believes that the poet must be at all times sincere. He must write about things that are important to him, and nothing is more natural than to be moved by something actually experienced: in fact, the experience and the reaction to it are one. Together, they are often the heart of her poetry.

That point of view is significant to Levertov herself is clear from her explanation:

I think that a poet has to be skilled and experienced before he begins using "I." He can come to it eventually; and I'm really beginning to let myself say "I" because I feel that now I can do it without the kind of crudity with which some people who have just begun to write poetry write about their own feelings.

I always feel that what such people should be doing, if they really want to be poets, is writing objectively. Writing about a chair, a tree outside their window. So much more of themselves really would get into the poem, than when they just say "I." The "I-ness" doesn't come across, because it's too crude, very often. For instance, the objective earlier poems of William Carlos Williams (who, in the ripeness of his old age has been saying "I" in a quite different way) say so much more than what they superficially appear to be saying. They're quite objective little descriptions of this and that, and yet, especially when one adds them together, they say a great deal about the man. In a much deeper, more impressive way than if he'd spend the same years describing his emotions. If a writer only describes how he feels, crudely, it's not very interesting. If he writes about the blackness of the sky and the dirtiness of the sidewalk, the experience is transferred, and we feel oppressed by these things, just as he did.[7]

Lest this discussion be oversimplified, let me add that some of the poems from *O Taste and See* are not written in first person. Most of the work dealing with nature, poetry, and personal relationships is in first person, and most of it ("Song for Ishtar," "Love Song," "About Marriage," "Hypocrite Women," "Our Bodies," "The Prayer," "Earth Psalm") is excellent. It is worth noting that some of the more obviously philosophic poems in this collection—"A March," "The Old Adam," "Shalom"—are less successful than some earlier poems, perhaps because Levertov is using the distance of third-person point of view. We can only wonder what might have resulted from a shift in perspective, had she written of not *you*, old Adam, but *I*.

Levertov's search for the inclusive poem has influenced her poetic structure as well as point of view. In 1958 appeared the first of her "sequence" poems, "Notes of a Scale" and "Scenes from the Life of the Peppertrees." Generally, the sequences are grouped under one title which indicates the thematic relationships, sometimes close, sometimes loose. The three poems of the peppertree poem, for example, are closely related: all are depictions of the tree's activity. Verbal techniques are similar in all, but the pace differs enough so that three separate poems are necessary. In other words, this sequence rhythmically could not have been written as a single poem. The title of the other poem mentioned, "Notes of a Scale," also suggests the situation: four short poems related through the implied subject, that of the magic inherent in any act of life, differ from one another insofar as vowel patterns and rhythm are concerned.

Levertov's later use of the sequence arrangement is more complex. In some poems, the counterpoint of rhythms or word patterns between sections of the poem proves to be a highly effective means of emphasizing content. Again, the variation on the given theme unites the group of poems. In 1965 Levertov suggested to a student who had written a long poem that she use the sequence form, if parts so created by this division would then cohere. Levertov felt that the sequence form is "valid—not merely an evasion of the need for a larger coherence—because of the varied material touched on."[8]

The sequence approach is at its simplest in the poems already mentioned and in "The World Outside," a poem made up of three scenes (and sounds) from the poet's New York apartment: each poem is separate, connected with the others through the motif of silence and a recurrent rhythm. Similarly, the distinctness of the poems in "Three Meditations" is emphasized by the use of separate epigraphs for each, but the motif of knowing oneself (and the figurative use of sounds, again) is the connecting thread. A like approach is evident in Levertov's controversial "During the Eichmann Trial," a three-poem sequence in which tone and subject of each differs greatly, but the implied theme is the same. Part I, "When We Look Up," depicts Eichmann (an Everyman figure) in his glass witness-stand, "a cage, where we may view/ourselves." Part II, "The Peachtree," is a suggestive account of a young boy's murder—for stealing fruit—at Eichmann's hands. These two poems are related by recurring images of the yellow star (representative of the Jewish faith as well as of Eichmann's own "light") coupled with the yellow peach being stolen and the frequent references to blood. Part II ends with these fine lines, focusing again on Eichmann rather than his victim:

> he would have enjoyed
> the sweetest of all the peaches on his tree
> with sour-cream
> with brandy
> Son of David
> 's blood, vivid red
> and trampled juice
> yellow and sweet
> flow together beneath the tree

> there is more blood than
> sweet juice
> always more blood—mister
> death goes indoors
> exhausted

Part III completes the poem by emphasizing the "always more
blood than/sweet juice" theme in a harsh account of "Crystal
Night":

> yes, now it is upon us, the jackboots
> are running in spurts of
> sudden blood-light through the
> broken temples . . .
>
> (*The Jacob's Ladder*, 65-66)

Although there is no direct mention of Eichmann in this last
poem, images like "blood-light" tie this section to the others; and
the final stanza draws the entire sequence together with the
reminder that all violence, all victimization, is only "a mirror/for
man's eyes."

No summary can re-create the power of this particular
sequence, a prime example of the effects possible when varying
tones and textures are juxtaposed to present one theme. Critics
who object that the poem does not approach the bestiality of
Eichmann, that he is treated with a ridiculous sympathy, may
well read the poem more carefully. The title of this poem is not
"The Eichmann Trial"; it is "*During* the Eichmann Trial"; and
as Levertov later writes in her notes to the poem, "The poem . . .
is not to be taken as a report of what happened but of what I
envisioned." One is reminded of William Carlos Williams' observation that every picture is in reality a self-portrait.

Levertov's emphasis on the important elements of tone, texture, and rhythm is illustrated in the sequence titled "Six Variations" (see pp. 69-70). The central theme is the naturalness of
man's tendency to create, the inherent "measure"/order in that
creation. Part I states the theme:

> We have been shown
> how Basket drank—
> and old man Volpe the cobbler
> made up what words he didn't know
> so that his own son, even
> laughed at him: but with respect.

The image of Basket, Gertrude Stein's dog, returns in Poem III as the dog's lapping of water "makes intelligent/music" and in Poem VI when the poet directs "Lap up the vowels/of sorrow." There are few recurring images in this sequence, partly because each poem is so rhythmically independent. Parts IV and V provide good illustration of this independence. They also provide good contrast within the poem. The following passages are marked to indicate the pauses and pace with which the poet read them in May 1962.

IV

When I can't'
strike one spark from you,'
when you don't'
look me in the eye,'
when your answers'
come'
    slowly,' dragging'
their feet,' and furrows'
change your face,'
when the sky' is a cellar'
with dirty windows,'
when furniture'
obstructs the body,' and bodies'
are heavy furniture coated'
with dust'—time'
for a lagging' leaden' pace,'
a short' sullen' line,'
measure'
of heavy' heart' and'
cold' eye.'

V

The quick of the sun that gilds'
broken pebbles in sidewalk cement'
and the iridescent'
spit, that defiles and adorns!'
Gold light in blind love does not
    distinguish'
one surface from another,' the
    savor'
is the same to its tongue,' the
    fluted'
cylinder of a new ashcan a dazzling
    silver,'
the smooth flesh of screaming
    children a quiteness,' it is all'
a jubilance,' the light catches up'
the disordered street in its apron,'
broken fruitrinds shine in the
    gutter.'[9]

As these pause designations show, Levertov arranges her lines and provides punctuation to good effect to enable the reader to re-create the intended rhythms of the poems. The relationship Levertov feels exists between the two devices—line division and punctuation—is indicated in her comment that "the line-end pause is a very important one which I regard more or less as equal to half a comma." Of the actual line length as an influence on pace, she writes: "Short lines mean more silences (line breaks) thus perhaps slowing the pace of the total poem, but pace *within the line* is determined by syllables, i.e., polysyllables ripple fast (in general) while monosyllables slow the line by their separation from each other. (Of course, pace is also determined to some extent by content, and the reader tends to make up for deficiencies in writing according to his own sense of the content.)"[10]

As if to illustrate her comment, she uses short lines in poem IV; consequently, the poem moves slowly. Often, subject or object is separated from verb, modifier from the word modified: such separation creates unexpected pauses (a kind of syncopation) even while the enjambment provides continuity of thought. A longer pause is created by the isolation of key words *measure* and *come*. The longer lines of Part V help to create more strident motion; again with much modified line enjambment. Part V contains only two sentences; Part IV, only one.

Apparently, as Levertov has pointed out, it is not only the line length, syntax, and punctuation marks that direct the tempo of these passages. It is the word selection itself. The adverbs and gerunds of the fourth poem, when coupled with many monosyllable word phrases ("when you don't/look me in the eye") and alliterative groupings ("lagging leaden"), make rapid reading impossible. Sibilants, long vowels, difficult consonants—all hamper facile movement, particularly when the syntactic pattern is a simple subject-verb.

In contrast, the plosives in the brittle words of Part V propel the reader through the extremely long phrases, as in the opening lines. The dominant vowel sound, long *i*, is usually pronounced quickly. Then too, the content of the passage is descriptive, focused on objects, whereas that of Poem IV depicts a personal relationship. The weight of the experience presented generally helps to determine pace, to at least some extent. As Levertov quotes from Edith Sitwell writing in her *Autobiography,* " 'not only structure, but also texture, are the parents of rhythm in poetry, and . . . variations in speed are the result, not only of structure, but also of texture.' "[11]

A consistent pace is one way of relating parts of the sequence poem, no matter how such pace is created. Many of Levertov's poem sequences are also connected through a constant theme and/or repetition of images—the yellow star-light-peach of the Eichmann poem, for example. The subject matter may be of a piece, as in "Claritas," "A Common Ground," or "A Ring of Changes"; or it may vary widely as in "Six Variations," "A Sequence," or "Matins." In "Matins," a morning song or prayer, the poet makes use of familiar morning scenes—a woman shutting off the alarm, a child eating breakfast, heat rising in the pipes. Yet the poem also contains many references to dream in general and to a Celtic legend in particular. Consequently, it is a difficult poem in its thematic concerns. An understanding of the pattern of juxtaposition used within it clarifies much of the meaning, however.

Dream is also the frame for the parts of "A Sequence," five poems based ostensibly on the poet's view of "A changing skyline." The poet, however, cannot make a simple statement; he cannot speak "flatly, 'as one drinks a glass of/milk' (for calcium)."

> Suddenly the milk
> spills, a torrent of black milk hurtles
> through the room, bubbling and
> seething into corners.

I quote this passage because it is typical of the near stream-of-thought association pattern used here and in other poems. The image of the qualifying simile ("as one drinks a glass of milk") becomes the subject of main action within the poem, the hurtling of milk-speech. Speech is not simple; neither is an identity: line 1 of Part II states, " 'But then I was another person!' " And just as speech cannot describe accurately ("images/split the truth/in fractions"), neither can the skyline be seen accurately. It is now "more/intensely designed, sprinkled/with human gestures" (see pp. 49-50).

Part II deals with these "human gestures"; Part IV, with the humanity (and the speech, silences, and memories) of the poet and her husband. Part V is an ostensible dream sequence, complete with an "absurd angel of happiness," gold cups, a pound of tomatoes. Ineffectual speech gives way at last to "naked laughter," a spontaneous communication despite the impermanence of all existence.

> Meanwhile the angel,
> dressed for laughs as a plasterer,
> puts a match to whatever's
> lying in the grate: broken scaffolds
> empty cocoons, the paraphernalia
> of unseen change.
> Our eyes smart from the smoke but
> we laugh and
> warm ourselves.
>
> (*The Jacob's Ladder*, 8-10)

Separate poems are united through the parallel and counter-pointed images of the recurring dreams, gold and blackness of milk, night, death. These poems show that the sequence structure is important because it permits room to elaborate on a theme. As she has said, and as her work shows, the unconscious area of realization is so valuable that the poet must have access to it. There must be space to wander, if wandering need occur.

Just as Levertov's poetic needs have brought her to this expansion of the limited lyric structure, so have they brought her to experimentation with movement through verbal patterns. One apparent outgrowth of her use of recurring words is an organization like that of "A Song," "Lonely Man," or "Clouds," an organization which might be called "madrigal." In music, the madrigal follows language rhythms rather than a fixed meter; it also contains sections dominated by varying moods, usually indicated by a key word within each. Most important, the structure is one of phrase repetition; the motifs overlap, with one voice bringing in a new theme while the rest are finishing the old. The movement of "Clouds" is in many ways similar to this description. Beginning with her personal description of clouds "surging in evening haste," she re-creates through the close word play a fear of death:

> Last night
> as if death had lit a pale light
> in your flesh, your flesh
> was cold to my touch, or not cold
> but cool, cooling, as if the last traces
> of warmth were still fading in you.
> My thigh burned in cold fear where
> yours touched it.

The fading warmth, the burning of her cold thigh foreshadow—
by means of words relating to cold and heat—the radiance to
come, in the harmony of nature:

> . . . a sky of gray mist it appeared—
> and how looking intently at it we saw
> its gray was not gray but a milky white
> in which radiant traces of opal greens,
> fiery blues, gleamed, faded, gleamed again,
> and how only then, seeing the color in the gray,
> a field sprang into sight, extending
> between where we stood and the horizon,
>
> a field of freshest deep spiring grass
> starred with dandelions,
> green and gold . . .
>
> (*The Jacob's Ladder*, 46)

Appearance-reality: the sky of cool gray is on closer view "not
gray but a milky white," accented with hot colors. And from the
sky to the field through the figure "starred," the bright earth
colors of dandelion accent the field. These passages culminate
in the poet's query, "Is death's chill . . . a gray to be watched
keenly?" and in her concluding statement that in man himself
lie "the colors of truth."

The early dominant tones of cool death and grayness merge
into the green-gold freshness of life, a reaffirmation which comes
as no surprise because of the words used in the earlier stanzas:
there is warmth amid the coolness; there is color amid the gray.
The same kind of progression is evident in "Love Song" and in
"Another Spring," as Levertov treats several themes within one
structure, blending the subjects rather than separating them as
she does in the sequence organization.

II *"Olga Poems"*

It is a commonplace of contemporary criticism that modern
poetic techniques are inadequate to sustain a long poem. What
modern epics exist—Pound's *Cantos*, Williams' *Paterson*, Hart
Crane's *The Bridge*, Eliot's *The Waste Land*, Charles Olson's
Maximus—have all been censured because of their "formlessness,"
their unevenness, or—at times—their sporadic applications of

technique. The question is, then, can modern poets write long poems? In Levertov's case, there is no epic as yet to judge. There is, however, the group of "Olga Poems," some two hundred lines of a single theme sequence written in memory of her sister, Olga Tatjana Levertoff, who died in 1964, aged forty-nine. It is Levertov's longest poem—at this time, one of her most recent— and it is interesting as an illustration of her means of sustaining a single subject.

Poem I, a succinct introductory song, is comprised of four short-line paragraphs in which the poet's older sister Olga lives in the poet's memory. Details accumulate as the poem progresses: the fire burns, the girl undresses, her skin is olive. The poet, then a child, watches from her bed, "My head/a camera." The poem concludes with a vivid contrast between the completeness of the young girl's body, and the fragmentation of that same body in death:

> Sixteen. Her breasts
> round, round, and
> dark-nippled—
>
> who now these two months long
> is bones and tatters of flesh in earth.

Poem II, more formal in its structure of short tercets, presents Olga's character more intensely—and that of the poet as well, in contrast. Although Levertov still uses much concrete detail ("the skin around the nails/nibbled sore"), it is detail integral to the type of personality described here—Olga at nine already filled with "rage/and human shame" at all injustice, herself often dealing unjustly with others in order to correct the initial wrong. The last stanza of this poem declares the recurrent theme, while reinforcing the image of the physically dark sister and that of the light already introduced in the fire passage:

> Black one, black one
> there was a white
> candle in your heart.

These preface poems are short and concise, the first written in paragraph format relying on visual presentation; the second, arranged in tercets and oriented toward Olga's character. Pace changes dramatically in Poem III. Itself a sequence of three longer segments, Poem III moves rapidly but gently. The long phrases are valid for two reasons: the poet is here speaking much more freely, with reminiscence woven into her direct commentary. Also, the interweaving motif of this sequence is "Everything flows," a line from the hymn, "Time/like an ever-rolling stream/bears all its sons away." The motion of this theme, of the actual words in it, demands a longer, more ostensibly accented line.

Part I of this sequence introduces the hymn concept, as the poet remembers its use in her earlier life. The second section shows Olga's dread of this concept of flow, of death. Some of her terror is reflected in the more restrained line arrangement here; although still long, lines now fall into tercets:

> But dream
> was in her, a bloodbeat, it was against the rolling dark
> oncoming river she raised bulwarks, setting herself
> to sift cinders after daily early Mass all of one winter, . . .
>
> To change,
> to change the course of the river! What rage for order
> disordered her pilgrimage—so that for years at a time
>
> she would hide among strangers, waiting
> to rearrange all mysteries in a new light.

The tercets continue in Part III, but lines are here short, helping to reflect a new intensity as the poet pictures her sister "riding anguish . . . over the stubble of bad years," "haggard and rouged," "her black hair/dyed blonde." The two concluding lines of this segment return somewhat ironically to the longer rhythms of earlier parts of this poem, and to the "Everything flows" theme. Now, however, it is said that Olga's life was "unfolding, not flowing." It appears, then, that the contrast between the grandeur suggested in the hymn and Olga's actual life—and death—is central to the poet's feeling as expressed through the poem.

Poem IV is another restrained poem before the rising rhythms of the concluding poems, V and VI. The short-line quatrains describe Olga's hospital life, hours of love and hate, pain and drugs quarreling "like sisters in you." In this poem return the images of the "kind candle" and the purifying flame, "all history/burned out, down/to the sick bone, save for/that kind candle."

Poem V, another sequence, moves again more slowly. Part I, in couplets, is dominated by images of gliding, winding, flowing—the poem thus is tied thematically and rhythmically with Poem III. These steady images, however, describe the *poet's* life as it was when both girls were young. There is momentary repose in this segment with its closing refrain, "In youth/is pleasure"; but the second poem returns to the painful life of an older Olga, buffeted by coldness "the year you were most alone."

Levertov achieves a vivid picture of Olga's desolation through images of frost and cold, loneliness, neglect, but perhaps even more effectively through the rhythms of this poem. Lines still are long, but they move more slowly because of monosyllabic words and word combinations difficult to articulate. The alliterative opening sets the pace for the poem:

> Under autumn clouds, under white
> wideness of winter skies you went walking
> the year you were most alone

Such lines as "frowning as you ground out your thoughts," "the stage lights had gone out," "How many books you read" lead to the closing tercet, which again depicts Olga as walking, but more than that: "trudging after your anguish/over the bare fields, soberly, soberly."

With a reference to "tearless Niobe," Levertov introduces the theme for the strongest poem in the group, the sixth. Light in various contexts (firelight, the light of memory, the candle) has been a central image throughout the poem—especially in contrast with the "black" elements, Olga herself and death. Levertov has used much visual detail, so that seeing has been important to the reader in the course of the poem. Now the eye itself is added to the accumulative image—and Olga's golden, fearful, mystery-filled eyes dominate Poem VI. Her eyes are the color of pebbles under shallow water, the water that flows throughout the poem. And in a very real sense her eyes are—for the fear of the moving water (representative, I assume, of the inherent flow from life to death) has colored Olga's life. Perhaps her eyes have always looked through this distorting mist. The remarkable thing about Olga's eyes, however, as the image pattern makes clear, is that they did remain alive, lit by "compassion's candle," even through their fear.

Levertov turns to the rhythms of blank verse in this most majestic part of the total poem. Poem VI is a continuation of the tone and movement established in the fifth, particularly in the second part, but the structure of the sixth poem is marked with an important difference—it is tightly connected through an interplay of the sounds which have been used at intervals throughout the poem—*l*'s, *s*'s, *o*'s—sounds which in themselves create a slow, full nostalgia. The final stanza of Poem VI incorporates these sounds, as well as the images and themes which have pervaded the earlier poems. The viewpoint reverts to that of the poet, but the tribute to Olga is clear:

> I cross
> so many brooks in the world, there is so much light
> dancing on so many stones, so many questions my eyes
> smart to ask of your eyes, gold brown eyes,
> the lashes short but the lids
> arched as if carved out of olivewood, eyes with some vision
> of festive goodness in back of their hard, or veiled, or shining,
> unknowable gaze . . .[12]

It is interesting that Levertov has included in this poem what recently appears to be one of her major poetic themes—the acceptance of change (even the last great change) as necessary to life. Olga's tragedy was an inability to accept that change. Her "rage for order" made her inflexible, even though "compassion's candle" burned through that inflexibility. This central theme was well expressed affirmatively five years earlier in "A Ring of Changes," the longest poem Levertov had written at that time. This poem is interesting technically as well as thematically. She uses a six-part arrangement, the first four short poems serving as prefaces. All four are in free paragraph form. The fifth poem is much longer; still in free form, it has longer lines. This central poem contains many symbols—the tree-vine of life, Casals' cello, a writer's worktable, light. It is a good poem, despite more didactic statement than in most of Levertov's poetry.

Yet "A Ring of Changes" as a whole is comparatively weak, I think, because it has no technical rationale. All the poems are separate, with few interrelating images or—perhaps more important to the poet—rhythms. Each poem is written in the same form; consequently, there seems to be little reason to divide the parts. The technical contrast between this poem and the Olga sequence is great.

The most critical reader cannot question the unity, the single effect, of the "Olga Poems"; yet Levertov's patterns of organization and rhythms differ widely within the poem. It is from her masterful use of contrast and balance that the harmony of the sequence comes—Poem IV, for example, slowing the movement, bringing the "everything flows" theme back to rest before it sets off again with new impetus.

It should be of interest to those critics who question the modern poets' technical proficiency that the techniques used throughout this long poem are the same devices Levertov uses in her short poems—the single-theme lyric, the sequence, the madrigal—each with its own appropriate line length and stanza arrangement. One fruit of her poetic experience is surely the unity of the "Olga Poems."

CHAPTER 6

'In Hope and Good Faith'

I *Worksheets as Illustration of Practices, "Olga Poems"*

CRITICISM by its very nature tends to establish arbitrary standards for judging poetry. Sometimes in speaking of organization, of prosody, of theme, the reader forgets that these segments are not separate from the poem as a whole—except as a convenience in the process of analysis. The poet does not think first of structure, then of words; he conceives of the poem as an entity. Perhaps in revision he considers separate elements in that, for example, he may change a word to strengthen rhythm. But writing poetry is seldom the orderly application of theories to practice that most critical discussions unfortunately suggest.

At issue here, I think, is the definition of the poetic process itself, a process which has been explored and described for centuries. That its mysteries have never been unraveled is, perhaps, a tribute to the innate power of the human spirit. For it seems to be agreed by nearly all poets, Levertov among them, that the poem begins somewhere in a non-intellectual response and is brought to perfection, finally, through a surveillance which is at least partly intellectual. As Levertov writes of Wallace Stevens' *mot*: " 'Poetry must resist the intelligence almost successfully.' *Almost*."[1]

Lest the poem sound entirely like a gift from a willfully evanescent muse, let me quote from her description of finding the impetus for poetry:

I have always disliked the idea of any kind of deliberate stimulation of creativity (from parlor games to drugs)—believing that if you have nothing you really feel, really must say, then keep your mouth shut; and I still believe that—but with a difference: Namely, that since I also believe that whatever in our experience we truly give our attention to will yield something of value, I have come to see that the *apparently arbitrary* focussing of that attention may also be *a way in* to our underground rivers of feeling and understanding, to revelations of truth.

Supervielle: "How often we think we have nothing to say when a poem is waiting in us, behind a thin curtain of mist, and it is enough to silence the noise around us for that poem to be unveiled."

Rilke: "If a thing is to speak to you, you must for a certain time regard it as the only thing that exists, the unique phenomenon that your diligent and exclusive love has placed at the center of the universe, something the angels serve that very day on that matchless spot."

I think what validates a practice or device which may otherwise only stimulate worthless, superficial, cynical work, is the writer's attitude when he uses it. If he works with "Kavonah" (care, awe, reverence, love—the "diligent love" Rilke speaks of) he can release the spark hidden in the dust.[2]

Levertov emphasizes that the poet must *attend* the poem, must "stay with the *prima materia* of a poem patiently but with intense alertness. As a result the language becomes active where in earlier stages it was sluggish. However, let me add that there are times when it is as important to know enough to keep one's hands off a poem—off a first draft that is right just the way it came—as to revise. Some 'given' poems arrive without any previous work (of course, unconscious psychic work has undoubtedly preceded them)."[3] The writer "has to look at the poem after he's written the first draft and consider with his knowledge, with his experience and craftsmanship, what needs doing to this poem. . . . It's a matter of a synthesis of instincts and intelligence."[4]

Since one of the paradoxes of art is the fact that some poems are "given" entire while others require more or less revision, this chapter consists largely of comparative excerpts from Levertov's worksheets. Through the example of the poet's own practice, I hope to identify her more common patterns in revision and, consequently, to add to knowledge of the craft of poetry.

Worksheets from the "Olga Poems" are interesting for various reasons. This particular group of poems poses the problem of controlling sentiment so that the poem is not obscured by too personal detail. In Poem IV, for example, the account of Olga's hospital life originally contained a reference to her fear of swimming, a biographical comment which seems irrelevant in this particular poem.

Early Version	Final Poem

. . . how you always
loved that cadence, 'Underneath
are the everlasting arms'—
You dreaded
the ocean—Father in ignorance
who could not swim,
thought to teach you by pushing
    you in
 	
all history
burned out, down
to the sick bone, save for
 	
that kind candle.[5]
	. . . how you always
	loved that cadence, 'Underneath
	are the everlasting arms'—
	all history
	burned out, down
	to the sick bone, save for
	
	that kind candle.
	        (*Poetry*, CVI, Nos. 1-2,
	        81-89.)

In early versions of Poem VI, the line "It was there I tried to teach you to ride a bicycle" has become, more appropriately, "I would . . . go out to ride my bike, return." The point to be made is that Olga is persistent, "savagely" so, in her playing; not that she needed instruction in bicycling.

Early Version

you turned savagely to the piano and sight-read
straight through all the Beethoven sonatas, day after day—
weeks, it seemed to one. I would turn the pages, some of the time.
It was there I tried to teach you to ride a bicycle.

Final:

you turned savagely to the piano and sight-read
straight through all the Beethoven sonatas, day after day—
weeks, it seemed to me. I would turn the pages some of the time,
go out to ride my bike, return—you were enduring in the
falls and rapids of the music . . .

In the final draft of the sixth poem again, personal emotion assumes what might be considered a more subtle expression.

Early Version:

> though when we were estranged,
> my own eyes smarted in the pain
>   of remembering you
>   as they do now, remembering
>   I shall never see you again

Final:

>   Even when we were estranged
> and my own eyes smarted in pain and anger at the thought of
> you.

Toward the end of the poem, the original line "gold brown eyes I shall never see again" becomes "gold brown eyes." To emphasize the finality of death, as in these early versions, is to mislead the reader at this point; for Levertov has further to go in her poetic re-creation. The central image of the late poems is of eyes, Olga's golden, mystic eyes—the candle image modified through implication. The closing impression of the poem sequence is not the poet's bereavement; it is rather Olga's unbroken character.

The sound pattern is particularly compelling in this last poem of the sequence. Yet in the early version, for all its contextual similarity, the pattern does not exist.

Early Version:

> Crossing the wooden bridge over the Roding
> where its course divided the open
> field of the present
> from the mysteries of the past,
> the old forest,
> I never forgot to think of your eyes
> which were the golden brown of
>   pebbles under the water,
> water under the sun.
> And crossing
> other streams in the world
> where the same light
> danced among stones
> I never forgot . . .

Final:
Your eyes were the gold brown of pebbles under water.
I never crossed the bridge over the Roding, dividing
the open field of the present from the mysteries,
the wraiths and shifts of time-sense Wanstead Park held
    suspended,
without remembering your eyes. Even when we were estranged
and my own eyes smarted in pain and anger at the thought of
    you.
And by other streams in other countries; anywhere where the
    light
reached down through shallows to gold gravel. Olga's brown
    eyes.

"where the same light/danced among stones/I never forgot . . ."
is very far, in sound, from "anywhere where the light/reached
down through shallows to gold gravel. Olga's/brown eyes." It
is interesting that Levertov has opened this final version with a
thought expressed almost as an aside in the earlier poem.

Similar modifications are evident in the ending of the poem.
The final impression is to be of Olga's calm yet unappeased
eyes. One early version of the poem ends,

. . . the lashes short but the lids
arched as if carved out of olivewood, eyes with some vision
of abundant and joyful life in back of them.

Rather than relying on the somewhat set adjectives, *abundant*
and *joyful*, the final version suggests the wealth, the ambiguity
of those very human eyes:

. . . the lids
arched as if carved out of olivewood, eyes with some vision
of festive goodness in back of their hard, or veiled, or shining,
unknowable gaze.

Often in revision the change is small—perhaps only a word or
two—but the effect is striking. I cite the closing lines of Poem V,
for example:

Early Version:
—Oh, in your torn stockings
    and unwaved hair
you were riding your anguish down
over the bare fields, soberly, soberly.

Final:

> Oh, in your torn stockings, with unwaved hair,
> you were trudging after your anguish
> over the bare fields, soberly, soberly.

For the passive, tearless Niobe, *trudging* is a better expression than *riding*. The same can be said of the changes made within Poem I. "The red waistband ring" of the final version was originally written as "itchy skin released from elastic reddened . . ."; objective detail must be not only accurate but consistent with the tone and movement of the poem. Tone may also have caused Levertov to delete the reference to "her kid sister's room" which appears in the original draft.

Many changes are made for the sake of emphasis. "I never forgot to think of your eyes" becomes "without remembering your eyes," a phrase much more positive in a grammatical sense. The movement of the latter phrase is also more suitable to the poem in which it appears, and rhythm in Levertov's poems is consistently an important consideration. For example, there are these lines from Poem V:

Early Version:

> . . . seeing again
> the signposts pointing to Theydon Garnon
> or Stapleford Abbots or Greensted
>
> crossing the ploughlands whose color I named 'murple'
> a shade between brown and lavender
> that we loved
>
> How cold it was in your thin coat,
> your down-at-heel shoes—

Final:

> . . . seeing again
> the signposts pointing to Theydon Garnon
> or Stapleford Abbots or Greensted,
>
> crossing the ploughlands (whose color I named *murple,*
> a shade between brown and mauve that we loved
> when I was a child and you
>
> not much more than a child) finding new lanes
> near White Roding and Abbess Roding, or lost in Romford's
> new streets where there were footpaths then—

frowning as you ground out your thoughts, breathing deep
of the damp still air, taking
the frost into your mind unflinching.
How cold it was in your thin coat, your down-at-heel shoes—

The addition of stanzas three and four in this selection helps to complete content as well as to provide rhythmic continuity. The fourth stanza bridges the earlier description of places in which Olga walked and the direct description to follow, of Olga as cold, alone, uncared for—but indomitable.

Aside from this revision, Levertov has made only very minor changes in this poem. Its companion poem, "In a garden grene whenas I lay," also remains very near the first draft. Worksheets in these cases prove, as the poet has said, that sometimes a poem "is right just the way it came." It is interesting that many of the first-draft poems ("Love Song," "Song for Ishtar," "Losing Track," "Song for a Dark Voice," as well as these from the Olga sequence) have a noticeable rhythm, a movement more intense than that of many other of her poems. "In a garden grene," for example, besides being song-like, makes use of phrases from a song as its theme.

One of the most interesting poems in the Olga sequence, so far as modification within versions is concerned, is the "Everything flows" passage of Poem III. In it, Levertov apparently knew some of "what she wanted to say" before she started; she was working from a poem concerning Olga begun many years earlier. Weaving together this early version, the quotation from the hymn, and her sense of the present poem to be written was difficult. As the final version of Poem III stands, Part I introduces the hymn phrase "Everything flows," relates it to the hymn context and Olga to the "human puppets," her actor friends. Part II re-creates the "alchemical" garden where the girls grew up, the poet's sense of her sister ("as if smoke or sweetness were blown my way"), and the underlying dread of life-change inherent in Olga's nature.

In early versions, however, the two divisions do not exist. All is one poem, and separate elements are arranged differently. The garden is mentioned early in the poem and in much detail; the "Everything flows" theme is mentioned, but it does not dominate the poem as it does later. It is probably this last point— the establishment of a key thematic phrase as the rhythmic heart of the poem—that makes the finished version work. The poem has a surging, re-surging motion (created by the suspended line endings and the use of silences, pauses) that is most appropriate to its theme. Early versions had no such controlling rhythm; they moved, in some places, much like prose. Indeed, Levertov marks them "notes for" the poem rather than drafts of it. Lines like

> the garden
> I grew in, a pilgrim cockleshell: alchemical square, trim thickets
> of flowers outlining length and depth, volcanic rocks in ordered
> latitiude . . .
> the same quaternal dream-place we thought at times was too small
> too trivial for our grand destinies . . .

become

> the garden, the same alchemical square
> I grew in, we thought sometimes
> too small for our grand destinies—.

Here certainly concentration is as important as rhythm. (What is relative here? Is this a poem about gardens?) But in the following excerpts, in which the original lines are expanded at times, rhythm seems to be more significant than any concern for economy. An early version reads,

> and again as if smoke or sweetness were blown my way for an
> instant
> I inhale the sense—with surprise, with unease—that you were
> feeling, were dreaming, were living your life there, young girl.

The later,

> Now as if smoke or sweetness were blown my way
> I inhale a sense of her livingness in that instant,
> feeling, dreaming, hoping, knowing boredom and zest like any-
> one else—
> a young girl in the garden

In another passage, shortened lines and better-chosen words make great improvement. The early version is written: "and the grass—at that time—recently trampled by the feet of your actors,/ the human puppets you used to assemble and drill into life— actors." The final version reads: "the trampled grass where human

puppets/rehearsed fates that summer,/stung into alien sem-
blances by the lash of her will—"

Beginning with *trampled* grass, Levertov in the final draft
suggests the struggle present in Olga's relationships with others,
intensified later by *stung* and *lash. Alien* helps to revivify the
somewhat overused puppet metaphor, as does the figure "re-
hearsed fates." An intermediate version of this passage is closer
to the final, but the phrasing is awkward:

> Pacing across the trampled lawn you were,
> where your actors, older than you but assembled and driven
> to intense semblances alien to them by your will's fury
> had rehearsed their parts.

So far as arrangement of the total poem is concerned, Poem
IV (the slow hospital sequence) and Poem V were reversed,
earlier. The present arrangement is more effective rhythmically:
the hospital passage provides needed contrast before the last
two poems build to the high pitch of the ending (see p. 118). As
Levertov's comments about the sequence form indicate, a poet
working with several elements may well have no preconception
of total form. Once the parts are written, he must then find the
most telling arrangement for the whole.

II   *Earlier Worksheets*

Levertov's earlier poem "A Sequence" is a good study of shift
in over-all organization. There are many differences between
arrangement in early versions and the final, partly because the
poet tends to condense and, in some cases, to delete passages.
Then too, subject matter is more homogeneous in this particular
poem—that is, several different passages contain references to
new buildings; several others, to dreams. Sections that are
separated in the final draft were once written as one, probably
because of these thematic ties (Poem III was the second part of
Poem IV in early drafts, for example).

The worksheets of "A Sequence" also reveal ways of attaining
juxtaposition, the abrupt positioning of seemingly independent
lines—conversations, dreams, descriptions—with little or no formal
transition. This near-montage arrangement supplants a chronological or logical order. Levertov has praised modern art for its

use of this technique because it has "found ways to juxtapose essentials and dispense with connectives."[6] She does so in "A Sequence." In early versions, for example, Poems I and II are connected with the line, "I hear myself say," followed by the explanatory statement,

> "But then, you must understand,
> I was another person.
> Now I am another person."[7]

The final draft has no connection line; the second stanza opens with only one line, " 'But then I was another person!' " Similarly, the connection between the poem's *persona* and the new building is explicitly stated in early drafts:

> I wore
> feathers of dream, as that building
> wears the blur of its scaffolds.
>
> Something obscured me
> from myself, as that building
> is blurred in its scaffolding.

and, somewhat later in the poem: "Well, just so I sloughed,/let's say, a veil/of scaffolds." The final version reads, " 'But then I was another person!'/The building veiled/in scaffolding."

Juxtaposition also aids in avoiding the restatements of theme that become, particularly in long poems, a kind of transition. In the final draft of Poem V, for example, the angel burns the "paraphernalia of unseen change" as the watching man and wife "laugh and warm" themselves at the fire. They survive as witnesses of change, and their recognition of this inevitable process closes the poem. In an earlier draft, this introspective passage is added: "Have we understood/nothing? Is anything solved?/Nothing is solved." This questioning changes the character of the poem greatly; it is deleted in later drafts. An intermediate version, more in the tone of the finished poem, relates the fire image directly to the scene of construction described early in the poem, through the mention of the couple's being warmed "each at the other's welcoming hearth, burning/on the volcanic stones the old/scaffolds, cocoons,/paraphernalia of unseen/change—good fuel."

The process of gaining more explicit phrasing through successive drafts of the poem is frequently illustrated in worksheets. Here, this series of openings for Poem V, the angel of happiness section. The first version opens "The morning brings/a dream joke. I wake up laughing." This opening poses problems, however, in that the fire-setting angel, the instrument of the necessary change, must be introduced somewhere. So a later draft reads: "Morning: an angel/came into the room, a box of/long matches in one hand." Another version adds description to the character of the angel.

> The morning: an angel
> comes into the room, in one hand
> a box of matches, in the other
> a book of dream jokes.
> It's the absurd
> angel of happiness.

The final poem attains even more of the angel's "absurdity," without the stage directions of time and place.

> But how irrelevantly
> the absurd angel of happiness walks in,
> a box of matches in one hand,
> in the other a book of dream-jokes.
>
> (*The Jacob's Ladder*, 8-10)

The poet has first added and then concentrated to achieve her desired impression, but the process of revision is never so arbitrary as this comment implies. Another interesting version from "A Sequence" is that of Poem II, where an "intruding" passage occurs. The four lines which are later deleted tend to turn the poem away from its immediate focus, the problem of inarticulation.

Early Version:

> Then say, 'From a silk mesh
> a creature slowly pushed out
> to stand clear—not a butterfly,
> some simply shaped, plainwinged, dayflying thing.'
>
> *Not enough.*

Final:

> *That's not enough.*
> Ah, if you've not seen it
> it's not enough.
> Alright.
> It's true.
> Nothing
>
> is even enough . . . .

Evidently Levertov recognized the lyric possibilities of the deleted lines, for they became the heart of a poem "The Disclosure," published in her last collection.

> From the shrivelling gray
> silk of its cocoon
> a creature slowly
>   is pushing out
> to stand clear—
>
>   not a butterfly,
>   petal that floats at will across
>   the summer breeze
>
>   not a furred
>   moth of the night
>   crusted with indecipherable
>   gold—
>
> some primal-shaped, plain-winged, day-flying thing.
>
> (*O Taste*, 61)

It is interesting that the primary features of the poem remain unchanged. More description is used; the verb tense changes from past to present; but the core of the poem is still "a creature slowly/is pushing out/to stand clear": "some primal-shaped, plain-winged, day-flying thing." As Levertov wrote in 1965, "material discarded from one poem may be the seeds of another."[8]

Most critics believe that a poet's worksheets are eminently valuable. In their differences as well as in their similarities, they provide a personal history of the creative process. They answer many questions even while posing others, like, why do some poems spring into life nearly whole while others require arduous reworking? One might say that it is partially a matter of length; fairly short poems can more easily be conceived in one time, although, of course, many short poems require as much work as the longer sequences. And for Levertov, at least, the frequency of "first-draft" poems has increased. It may well be that the particular kind of concentration that produces the entire poem can also be cultivated and developed, as can many kinds of intellectual prowess.

Conclusively, worksheets show little except that there is no formula for writing a good poem. There are only very general rules of reconsidering the often ephemeral first draft. A few of these, evident in the poet's worksheets, are the deletion of extremely subjective passages, or didactic expressions of idea, and extraneous words and phrases—an excess modifier, an unnecessary transition. But concentration, "intensification," is never a simple process, as Levertov explains:

> "Intensifying" on a rudimentary level is often simply a matter of going through a poem looking for words that can be eliminated without losing anything necessary.
>
> But more deeply than that, we *intensify* if we remember to *sing* rather than to talk. Or rather, even if our desire and intention is to write narrative poems, dramatic poems, discursive poems, it will always be well not to let ourselves forget that poetry's deepest root is in incantation and that it is closely and anciently allied to music. *The closer to song the texture of any kind of poem, the more deeply expressive it will be.*[9]

Then, too, because expansion is frequently a means of clarifying or emphasizing, not all Levertov's finished poems are shorter than their first versions. Particularly in her late poetry, the musical requirements of the poem often demand not only expansion, but also the addition of entire passages. The practice of poetry seems to be a career of exceptions.

For this very reason, that the process of the poem does vary so much, Levertov—like many other poets—has come to consider the poet partially as instrument, as vehicle, for the creation of the poem. The very choice of these words, however, implies the skills which poets themselves must have once the poem has been "given."

CHAPTER 7

'Dialogue with His Heart'

I *The Unity of the Diverse*

The true artist: capable, practicing, skillful;
maintains dialogue with his heart, meets things with his mind.

("The Artist," *With Eyes*, 4)

A MAN who once wrote good poetry told me that he gave up his writing because his work was not individual enough— not recognizable as being truly his. This dilemma is an extension of a premise generally accepted in literature—that the writing of the master artist will be identifiable because of themes and techniques peculiar to it. The premise is partly inductive: one can recognize the novels of Charles Dickens, the plays of Shakespeare, the poems of William Blake. But the premise is also partly subjective, I think, for it is based on a belief in the artist's complete honesty and in the stability of his goal. The assumption is that even in the most highly charged atmosphere of change, of catastrophe, the good writer maintains direction.

Perhaps we assume too much. However, the point does remain—more or less given—that the works of one writer will be characteristic and, furthermore, will be in some ways interrelated. Levertov has great praise for "the reverberation of the total" within even the short poems of William Carlos Williams, "so that every poem is at once a complete thing . . . and at the same time relates to all your other poems. . . . this is one of the marks of greatness, this unity of the diverse."[1] In the exposition for *Poet's Choice*, Levertov describes the impossibility of choosing a single "favorite" poem because each one is part of "the larger poem that is a lifetime's work-in-progress." Even the poet cannot see the entire design—or, consequently, evaluate his work fully—until his career is finished.[2] This is particularly true of a poet like Levertov who considers the poem "a *voyage* (of discovery) rather than *statement* (of what you already know)."[3]

As I have tried to show in previous chapters, Levertov's poetry meets this criterion of the unified "larger poem"—in its reciprocal themes, its characteristic rhythms, and its technical similarities. Not only can correspondences be found among most of her recent poems; her early British work, often disregarded as inferior, also relates to these continuing patterns. So too does much of her prose. And even her choice of poems for translation appears to be compatible with her full poetic rationale.

The poems of Levertov's first published book, *The Double Image*, are in many ways characteristic—despite the technical influence of traditional English poetry. Although this collection was published in 1946, some eleven years before her first American book, the pervasive themes are already evident—man's essential separateness, but also his great promise of fulfillment through love, self-knowledge, and dream ("Listening to rain around the corner/we sense a dream's reality"). The exuberance of *O Taste and See* is already present: "The air of life is music, and I live." Point of view is somewhat different, however, in that the poet is not speaking to others of her own experiences (as in nearly all her later poems); she is rather urging herself on to these experiences.[4]

In the central "Autumn Journey," for example, Levertov describes the passive "wanderer" who has been resting in "comfortable myth and drowsy mansion." She urges him to leave the "soft forgetful murmur" of his flowers and their "mirrored doubles." (This image, suggesting the title of the book, is relevant in that the "double image" occurs only when life/water is tranquil, perhaps too tranquil. In its ambiguity also the phrase suggests a blurred vision. Like the titles of many of her books, this one is again concerned with sight.) As the poem concludes, the wanderer must journey "among the burning worlds" in order to find life's treasure. In "To Death," Levertov enumerates a miscellany of this "treasure":

> These leaves of lightness and these weighty boughs
> that move alive to every living wind,
> dews, flowers, fruit, and bitter rind of life,
> the savour of the sea, all sentient gifts
> you will receive, deserve due ritual;[5]

Both this catalogue and the themes of these two poems parallel her later poem, "O Taste and See."

These, then, are the days of eager anticipation, of "life-green fires," even in the midst of World War II. There are few poems about war in this book, and those few characteristically portray the concepts of hate and fear obliquely:

> but on the plains of childhood where the deer
> grazed undisturbed on amber afternoons
> lay already the shadow of starving snow,
> the first signs of fear.

> ("'One There Was,'" *The Double Image,* 25)

The emphasis is instead on man's ability to fulfill—love as "a candle to dazzle the day"—and confidence in nature: "I hear no menace in the wind;/the tree is mine, and grows about my heart." Love must color the world, even though, as Levertov writes in the opening of "Fable,"

> There still are forests we must penetrate,
> dark as silence and stricken suddenly
> with scream of bright birds caught by flesh-eating flowers
> and where the river green as tarnished gold
> flows in slow thunder to unruffled lakes . . .

> (*The Double Image,* 40)

Technically, perhaps, many of these poems could be called "derivative." There is often the pattern of quatrain or tercet, or the paragraph in blank verse. There is sometimes a use of alliteration for its own sake; of the obvious simile, perhaps as filler for a short line; of excessive modifiers and classical allusions. Particularly among the early poems in the book, the abstract is frequently the subject (the "stony slope" of Time). Clarity is sometimes sacrificed to the requirements of set form.

Because of instances of this type of weakness within a few poems, critics tend to overlook *The Double Image,* stressing in their dismissal the fact that Levertov's poetic style was so greatly changed after her arrival in America that her early poetry is incidental. I cannot agree with this appraisal. Too many of the poems in *The Double Image* prove otherwise: that even though the atmosphere of America may have brought Levertov's talents to fruition, her early work is itself a rich beginning. It might well be said that Levertov's mature poetic style would have been impossible to achieve without both areas of experience, the English and the American.

Her emphasis on sounds within the poem, for example, is certainly evident in this 1945 poem, "Days":

> This day has no centre; it flows, blows,
> like scents of a drowsy summer heath
> or hesitant snows that glide,
> silent as owls' wing, down to a silent field.
> Yesterday was cut in stone, was bone
> firm under flesh, inevitable line
> of limb and purpose, hard
> as a star's radiance, cold as a cold desire . . .
>
> (*The Double Image*, 36)

In these two stanzas Levertov uses the dominant sound patterns so well that the movement of each stanza differs; the "flows, blows,/like scents of a drowsy . . ." establishes smooth sonority in contrast to the more abrupt motion of the second stanza. Tone differs also, even though one of the principal vowel sounds in both passages is the long *o*. In this poem too, she works with the careful repetition of key single words: *silent* in the first stanza; *cold* in the second; *love* in the conclusion. (The technical similarity between this poem and "Resting Figure" from *The Jacob's Ladder* should be noticed.)

This interest in repeated words, or various forms of one word, is illustrated in "To the Inviolable Shade," with its repetition of *pain, world,* and *lost-loss:* "The pain of the world is in the air we breathe:/tender satirical lover of the lost,/no pain but your loss can darken all my world" (*The Double Image*, 11). Word arrangement is much more successful here than it is in "Dreams," where the first and fourth lines of each stanza end with the same word. Evidently Levertov is experimenting with all types of word patterns, some very conscious, others seemingly more spontaneous. Several poems make use of a formal refrain. "Casselden Road," for example, contains the refrain "No one else/ will remember this. No one else will remember." In tone and pace, this particular refrain is very close to that of Levertov's 1965 poem, "A Lamentation": "Grief, have I denied thee?/Grief, I have denied thee."[6]

Because many of these early poems are written in traditional stanza forms, Levertov must choose her words with some consideration of expected rhyme and rhythm patterns. She can, however, seldom be charged with "padding." She is not afraid to write irregular lines; and there is some evidence that she is already interested in the pause as a component of the active line. Occasionally, too, she creates original stanza forms which are maintained throughout a poem, as in " 'They, Looking Back, All th' Eastern Side Beheld' ":

> Now I travel on another road
> climbing the long hill to a weary town,
> but still sometimes
> when fragile laughter breaks
> I know the gold, the gold,
> of Shelley's orange weighty as the world.

(The Double Image, 10)

Movement within this stanza appears to be very free, yet she is adhering to a set six-line, variable accent pattern. Part of her success comes from a sparing use of modifiers—*long, weary,* and *fragile*—and an active syntax which builds to the poet's joy in knowing "the gold, the gold." The dominance of long vowels in the *l-s* pattern foreshadows what is to become a characteristic Levertov tone. These are lines of mature poetry, regardless of when or under whose influence they were written.

II *The Relationship of Prose*

In many cases, Levertov's prose is also marked by her distinctive tone and pace. Prose rhythms are often based on long periodic sentences, broken by appositives or series into easily spoken phrases and accented at times by short sentences. For example, this opening paragraph from her prose poem, "A Dream": "A story was told me of the sea, of time suspended as calm seas balance and hover, of a breaking and hastening of time in sea tempest, of slow, oil-heavy time turning its engines over in a sultry night at sea. The story belonged not to time but to the sea; its time and its men were of the sea, the sea held them, and the sea itself was bounded by darkness" (*With Eyes,* 54).

The near-Biblical pace is maintained throughout the full account of the strangely united sailors, Antonio and Sabrinus. The story of their loves and hates has a definite narrative force, in spite of the deliberate movement, a movement resulting from the long sentences (the opening paragraph contains only two, and each of those has at least one series). Important, too, in establishing tempo is the repetition of the central nouns, *sea* and *time*. *Sea* appears eight times in the short paragraph; *time*, five. The variation in each word's usage (as subject, object, or object of preposition) adds contrast; primarily the reader is intended to feel the weight of these words—the timelessness of time, the darkness bordering the mysterious sea. Like the nuances of a poem, individual phrases create differing rhythms within the pervasive movement: "of time suspended as calm seas balance and hover" which is a slow line because of long vowels and extended syllables; "of a breaking and hastening of time in a sea tempest" in which plosives move these more active and, in some cases, polysyllabic words faster; and "of slow oil-heavy time turning its engines over in a sultry night" which moves slowly because of longer vowels and less active syntax; i.e., more modifiers.

"A Dream," which seems to be reminiscent of a Hasidic tale or Biblical prose, is more formal—its pace more controlled—than is "A Note on the Imagination"; but the writing in each is similar in sentence arrangement and general technique. These prose pieces foreshadow Levertov's first published short story, "Say the Word," praised by Godfrey John as being one of "the most beautiful poems in *O Taste and See*."[7] Although "Say the Word" differs in structure from the shorter prose, its rhythm is again similar:

> She stood as if unable to move, crossing her arms tightly as the evening grew colder. Her husband was full of a new liveliness these days. He moved from his desk to the fields and back again with a new lightness, as if such transitions were easy or as if there were no question of transition, as if the use of the mind and the use of the body were all one rhythm. She knew that was good, that was the way life should be lived. Could she—with her persistent sense of the precariousness of happiness, the knife-edge balance of his confidence, of all sureness—could she run to him now with a plea to stop what she had begun?
>
> (*O Taste*, 45-46)

The short sentences heighten the pace of the long units, and again Levertov uses restatement, series, apposition.

"Say the Word" is a simple story of a woman, a man, their son, living on an old farm, making of it a home. Like "A Dream," it is a story of man's need to realize his humanity. The woman wants the tree cut down so that she can satisfy her need, to see the far mountains. Yet she dreads the death of the tree; in killing it a violence is being done the dignity, the form, of nature. In this excerpt which describes the woman waiting for the tree to fall, Levertov emphasizes again the images of sound, motion, and color which dominate the prose:

> There was a pause. A murmur of voices, the tree seeming to hold its breath. The woman brushed away insects that were biting her bare legs and buzzing around her ears. Another phrase came from the thrush, from further away. The colors were gone from the sky now; the light that remained was toneless. All the varied greens of the woods had become a single dull green. . . . She remained where she stood, sullenly enduring the biting of the flies and mosquitoes that had gathered around her, not even trying to wave them away with a piece of bracken.
>
> (46)

The theme—man as he who decides—is not new to Levertov's work. Cutting down the poplar becomes a decisive act, is, in fact, making a *clearing*. A flashback to a neighboring farm, now abandoned, implies that nature needs humane control; the sight of the farm is depressing because its "horizon" is "blocked." Man needs the open horizon, the sight of the mountains.

This concern with man's being, with his values, is evident throughout Levertov's work. Most of her translations are of poems concerned in some way with the human condition, particularly those of Jules Supervielle and the Vaishnava, Indian religious poems. In her literary criticism, Levertov's reactions to an artist's work are also frequently on moral grounds rather than on purely technical ones. She praises Gilbert Sorrentino's poems because "He has a moral force, a kind of angry pride as if he had been much hurt but never drowned. . . ."[8] Of Robert Lax she writes, "the radiant security of his faith appears in his work as a serenity of tone."[9] Jack Gilbert's poetry is "original and authentic" because his is "a new voice speaking in its own way—urgent, carrying a sense of pain and pride."[10]

And she respects the "sober truthfulness" of David Ignatow's poems, of which she writes: "They are written with a proud, simple refusal of whatever is not 'proven on his pulses.' One sees that he took up the challenge of an 'ordinary,' a somewhat drab, life and resolved to make his poetry out of that or not at all: from its exigencies, from an ordinary job, from ordinary grief, ordinary worry, ordinary deep, sad, difficult love."[11] As was apparent in her review of Edith Sitwell's *Autobiography* (see p. 19), she feels that any insincerity destroys qualities inherent to the poem. In contrast to her censure of Miss Sitwell, Levertov has reverent praise for "the largely unconscious, all-embracing sincerity of great artists whose whole being stands doggedly in back of their work."[12] Her prose and poetry show that she merits inclusion in her own description.

III *"Influences"*

No study of a writer is complete, at least in this age of the literary super sleuth, without some discussion of work which has influenced him. Few poets write in a vacuum; most are amazingly literate people whose response to the written word has fostered their own abilities. Several poets have been or are important in Levertov's poetic development.

Levertov's respect for William Carlos Williams' work has frequently led critics to think Williams a dominant influence. They cite his insistence on an "American language" as being central to Levetov's later poetry. Her answers to his persuasions on that point have been discussed (see p. 29), but she undoubtedly considered his views in the formulation of her own.

Others see in her earlier poems, like "Merritt Parkway" and "The Hands," Williams' interest in capturing the object visually, his demand for concrete detail. So far as it goes, this comment is accurate; but it should be noted that much other contemporary American poetry illustrates this approach. Probably the poems in *Here and Now* and *Overland to the Islands* are those most reminiscent of Williams' own earlier techniques—"The Way Through," "Pure Products." In the past decade, however, changes have occurred within Levertov's poetry, changes that have taken most of her work far from that first kind of Williams' influence. As Thom Gunn explains the possible relationship between Levertov and Williams,

To learn from him, even to imitate him, is not to be dominated by his thought or mannerisms . . . for Williams has few mannerisms, and his power over rhythm and image is not matched by a power over ideas. His world is one of innumerable accurately recorded perceptions loosely grouped around certain personal emotions, and it is his accuracy of perception rather than any principle in the grouping that makes him a model for imitation.

Gunn feels that Levertov is "fully individual, even though her *outlook* is often very similar to his."[13]

I think too that the most significant influence Williams had on Levertov lies in the area of theme. Too many readers have not yet read Williams' best poems, those written after 1950; they do not realize that Williams was the humanist—or, better, humanitarian—*par excellence* of poetry; and that it is his great love which the late poems finally express. Perhaps this quality of unashamed revelation of emotion in poems like "Asphodel" encourages Levertov in her own choices of theme. Her letters to Williams are seldom about "technique." They deal primarily with the sentiments, the human concern, of Williams' work. Technically, the older poet did insist again and again that Levertov cut, file, condense. His comments undoubtedly forced her to reconsider her poetry, but they were hardly the chief reason Levertov admired Williams and his poems so much.

So far as poetic technique is concerned, Wallace Stevens and, more incidentally, Hilda Doolittle, are probably the most important poets to Levertov. The emphasis on sound is primary (as Levertov describes poetry as having its origin in "incantation and music").[14] But also, the subtle effects from the wonderfully ambiguous word, the joy in a line whose rhythm parallels its thought, the counterpoint of contrasting moods which again reflect content—these are properties of Stevens' poetry which are rare in contemporary work except, to a lesser degree, in H.D.'s; and increasingly, in Levertov's and Robert Duncan's.

Thematically, too, there is a richness in the work of Stevens that cannot be compared with the objective mode prevalent today. Levertov writes of this characteristic as illustrated in the poems of Hilda Doolittle:

H.D. spoke of essentials. It is a simplicity not of reduction but of having gone further, further out of the circle of known light, further in towards an unknown center. . . . She showed a way to penetrate mystery; which means, not to flood darkness with light so that darkness is destroyed, but to *enter into* darkness, mystery, so that it is experienced. And by *darkness* I don't mean evil; not evil but the Other Side, the Hiddenness before which man must shed his arrogance. . . .[15]

It is not only the inclusion of the past, of mystery, or the poet's use of prose as a means of achieving this wider inclusion of person; rather, the entire philosophy of inclusion is important to Levertov's work. Just as Stevens brings into "Peter Quince at the Clavier" color, sound, touch, and the primitive respect for virtue, so does Levertov draw from dream, sensuality, objective response, autobiography—any subject that seems relevant so long as the poet is working honestly. Levertov describes the poem's power to include as its "generosity, its large capacity, the way the unique history of a poem can be incorporated into its structure, and that that history may itself include rifts, faults like geologic faults, unresolved mysteries, mysteries as rites and powers, and also what appears to be clutter, even, but is not obstructive clutter but something akin to the energetic diversity of the natural world."[16]

Levertov is speaking in the above excerpt not of H.D. or Stevens but of what Robert Duncan has taught her. Duncan, one of the most respected of contemporary poets, admits his admiration for, particularly, H.D. His use of melody and the wide inclusion of his themes, evident in the Venice poems and other sequences from *Roots and Branches,* has probably reinforced the impact of these earlier poets on Levertov; for of all poets contemporary with her, she most respects Duncan. As she said in her introduction to their 1964 reading at the Guggenheim Museum, "His poetry and his thinking and the range of his knowledge have been for me an element so pervasive that it is difficult to describe."[17]

Robert Creeley also has been important to Levertov's work, partly at least for his insistence on unimpaired movement. As she writes of Creeley in the early 1950's, "he showed me *how* and *why* to cut."[18] And Creeley, with his deep respect for the work of Williams and Ezra Pound, encouraged her interest in these writers.

Important too are the letters and poetry of Kenneth Rexroth. Rexroth, in whose collection *New British Poetry* Levertov had her first American publication, wrote to her while she was still in England (1946). His letters helped her choose the American and European writers whose work was most meaningful to her. Then, also, Rexroth's own *The Signature of All Things* was valuable.

These are some of the poets whom Levertov admires. It is no secret that she respects their poetry, but her own is unlike any of theirs. Her work is neither eclectic or imitative. As I have tried to show throughout this book, Levertov's poems have such a characteristic tone, pace, and thematic focus that they constitute a whole. Perhaps one might say, then, that these "influences" have stimulated existing propensities instead of forcing alterations. They may be viewed as having given more encouragement than they have knowledge. To any consideration of influences, also, should be added the writing of Tennyson, Keats, Spender, Auden, and the Elizabethan lyricists; Rilke's poetry and letters; the Hasidic legends; and fairy tales. Even then, there appears to be no formula for the poetry presently written by Denise Levertov.

Perhaps a reader, keeping in mind these briefly noted influences for whatever they are worth, might listen with more profit to these comments from Miss Levertov herself, as she instructs young writers in a seminar on the craft of poetry:

1. Remember Mallarmé's words that "Poems are not made with ideas, they are made with words."

2. Beware of consciously searching for the original; nothing is more likely to lead to the banal. The *fresh* word is not necessarily the *odd* word.

3. Keeping a notebook, translating from other languages, setting aside a time each day to be alone and think about poetry, are ways of making a place for possible poems.

4. Keep in mind the distinctions between speaking and singing, walking and dancing. Valéry says: "we note that in song the words tend to lose their importance as meaning, that they do most frequently lose it, whereas at the other extreme, in everyday prose, it is the musical value that tends to disappear; so much so that song on the one side and prose on the other are placed, as it were, symmetrically in regard to verse, which holds an admirable and very delicate balance between the sensual and intellectual forces of language."

5. Don't think of any element of poetry—such as rhythm—as a discrete phenomenon. Do try always to bear in mind the organic relationship each element in a good poem must have to every other element. None is an external factor to be applied.

6. A poem does not merely present or describe certain facts; it instead relates them to one another, or rather, implies their relation to one another and the relation of "facts" to "feelings."

7. D. H. Lawrence wrote, in an essay called "Life": "Who can say, Of myself I will bring forth newness? Not of myself, but of the unknown which has ingress into me."

8. Strength of feeling, reverence for mystery, and clarity of intellect must be kept in balance with one another. Neither the passive nor the active must dominate, they must work in conjunction, as in a marriage.[19]

These instructions echo and extend Levertov's description of "The Artist," quoted earlier in this chapter, "The true artist: capable, practicing, skillful;/maintains dialogue with his heart, meets things with his mind." One is struck with the applicability of this definition to Levertov herself. Her past writing has already proved the constancy of her desire, the freshness of her perception, the viability of her poetic gifts: her identity as "true artist."

Notes and References

Chapter One

1. Denise Levertov, *Overland to the Islands* (Highlands, North Carolina, 1958), p. 24. Hereafter cited as *Overland.*
2. Denise Levertov speaking as panelist at University of British Columbia poetry seminar, August, 1963.
3. From "Poem as Counterforce: Responsibilities and Possibilities," typescript in Miss Levertov's personal collection.
4. From notes made by Miss Levertov as reader on the manuscript of *The Poems of William Carlos Williams: A Critical Study.*
5. Cited in David Ossman, *The Sullen Art* (New York, 1963), pp. 75-76. Mr. Ossman's interview with Miss Levertov.
6. Notes from "The Craft of Poetry," a seminar given by Miss Levertov at The Poetry Center, New York, from October 1964 to February 1965.
7. "Monster with Melopoeia," *The Nation,* CC (June 7, 1965), 619.
8. Notes from "The Craft of Poetry" seminar.
9. Remarks made at University of British Columbia, 1963.
10. See "H.D.: An Appreciation," *Poetry,* C (June, 1962), 182-86.
11. "'The Arena Where We Fight,'" *The Nation,* CXCVII (December 21, 1963), 440.
12. From "Art (After Gautier)," *With Eyes at the Back of Our Heads* (Norfolk, Conn., 1960), p. 73. Hereafter cited as *Eyes.*
13. "Statement on Poetics," *The New American Poetry, 1945-1960,* ed. Donald M. Allen (New York, 1960), p. 412.
14. Levertov does, however, admire this poem of Ginsberg's because she thinks the poet is truthful about his emotion, and therefore, the poem works.
15. "Total Individual Responsibility," *Midwest,* Nos. 5-6 (Spring, 1963), 19.
16. "Poets, Old and New," *Assays* (Norfolk, Conn., 1961), p. 232.
17. John Napier, "A Brace of Beatniks," *Voices,* CLXXIV (January-April, 1961), 48.
18. *"With Eyes at the Back of Our Heads,"* San Francisco Chronicle (February 28, 1960), p. 22.

19. "Denise Levertov: Poetry of the Immediate," *Tri-Quarterly*, IV, No. 2 (Winter, 1962), 34-35.

20. "Gravity and Incantation," *The Minnesota Review*, II (Spring, 1962), 424.

21. Among Paul Levertoff's published works are the following: *The Lambeth Appeal for Re-Union* and *Old Testament Prophecy and the Religions of the East*, in Russian; *Life of Saint Paul, The Religion of Israel, The Son of Man, The Christian Doctrine of God*, and a translation of the *Confessions of St. Augustine*, in Hebrew; *Hassidism*, in German; *Love and the Messianic Age, Commentary on Saint Matthew, Saint Paul in Jewish Thought*, a translation of *Paul among the Jews, Hebrew Christian Liturgy in Hebrew and English*, a translation of *Jesua-Jeshua*, and *Synagogue Worship in the Time of Christ*, in English.

22. *Tales of the Hasidim: The Early Masters* (New York, 1947), p. 3.

23. Original typescript of Walter Sutton's "A Conversation with Denise Levertov," appearing in *The Minnesota Review*, V, No. 3-4 (December, 1965).

24. *O Taste and See* (Norfolk, Conn., 1964), p. 66. Hereafter cited as *O Taste*.

25. Francis G. Wickes, *The Inner World of Choice* (New York, 1963), p. 30.

26. Personal correspondence with the poet, 1963.

27. "Biographical Note," Allen's *New American Poetry*, p. 440.

28. Levertov's letter to William Carlos Williams, dated only September 21. Letter refers to a poem published in 1961. From the Yale University Library American Literature Collection, Dr. Williams' letters.

29. "Biographical Note," Allen's *New American Poetry*, p. 441.

30. Personal correspondence, November, 1965.

31. September 21 letter, Yale Collection. It was soon after this exchange of letters, however, that Miss Levertov was visiting Dr. Williams at his home, and he told her that he had come to like the poem and asked that she read it to him no fewer than four times.

32. *The Jacob's Ladder* (Norfolk, Conn., 1961), p. 37.

33. ". . . Individual Responsibility," p. 18.

34. "Some Simple Measures in the American Idiom and the Variable Foot," *Pictures from Brueghel* (Norfolk, Conn., 1962), p. 47.

35. Personal correspondence with Robert Creeley, letter dated May 29, 1964.

36. Sutton interview, p. 323.

37. "Necessary Poetry," *Poetry*, XCIII (November, 1960), 108.

38. "Rhythms of Speech," *New York Times Book Review* (June 21, 1964), p. 12.

39. "Statement on Poetics," Allen's *New American Poetry*, pp. 411-12.

Chapter Two

1. Quoted as epigraph to Poem ii of "Three Meditations," *The Jacob's Ladder*, p. 30.

2. "An Admonition," *things*, No. 1 (Fall, 1964), 4-5.

3. "H.D.: An Appreciation," p. 186.

4. "Necessary Poetry," p. 104.

5. "Asking the Fact for the Form," typescript of Wabash College Lecture (December 6, 1962), p. 2.

6. "'An Order That Will Sing,'" *The Nation*, CXCII (May 13, 1961), 417.

7. "Asking the Fact for the Form," p. 1.

8. At University of British Columbia, Vancouver, British Columbia. The title comes, as Levertov also mentioned then, from the Hasidic belief that everything holds sparks of the divine, sparks which are awaiting redemption. As she writes in "The Necessity" (*O Taste*, 56), "each part/of speech a spark/waiting redemption."

9. Personal letter, 1963.

10. "A Note on the Imagination," *New Directions 17* (1961), p. 50.

11. *Here and Now* (San Francisco, 1957), 28.

12. "Come into Animal Presence," *The Jacob's Ladder*, 21.

13. Quoted as epigraph to "The Part," *The Jacob's Ladder*, 6.

14. "Asking the Fact for the Form," pp. 2-3.

15. Introduction to Russell Edson's *The Very Thing That Happens* (Norfolk, Conn., 1964), p. vi.

Chapter Three

1. Note to "The Runes," *O Taste*, 83.

2. Original typescript for Sutton's interview.

3. The concept of rebirth may have more meaning in the Jungian sense, as Francis Wickes describes it: "The moments when the soul awakens to reality are moments of 'man's opportunity to be blessed.' They are true experiences of rebirth. The 'whole man,' the 'real man,' is, not the once-born or the twice-born, but the one continuously reborn in the eternal process of becoming and of being. Every moment of new awareness which is confirmed by the self in total experience is rebirth" (*The Inner World of Choice*, p. 309).

4. "Necessary Poetry," p. 109.

5. "Statements on Poetics," Allen's *New American Poetry*, pp. 386-400.

6 "Some Notes on Organic Form," *Poetry*, CVI, No. 6 (September 1965), 424.

7. As Levertov has pointed out in personal correspondence (November, 1965), her lines are never entirely run-on. The break at the end of a line is always intended as a pause, equal in time value to "roughly one-half a comma and modified variously by such factors as punctuation and the position of strong accents in the line just finished and in the line to come."

Chapter Four

1. Sutton interview, pp. 328-329.

2. "Poets of the Given Ground," *The Nation*, CXCIII (October 14, 1961), 252.

3. *Ibid.*, p. 253.

4. Notes made as a reader on the manuscript of *Williams*.

5. "Asking the Fact for the Form," p. 4.

6. *Ibid.*

7. It should be noted that Levertov uses this word in the sense of "the nature of something" rather than as nature *per se*.

8. "Play with Words," *The Nation*, CXCVIII, No. 6 (February 3, 1964), 126.

9. "Asking the Fact for the Form," p. 6.

Chapter Five

1. As quoted by Charles Olson in his "Statement of Poetics," Allen's *New American Poetry*, p. 387.

2. University of British Columbia poetry seminar discussion, August, 1963.

3. "Asking the Fact for the Form," with some sections taken from the adaptation of this lecture which appeared as "Some Notes on Organic Form."

4. Notes from "The Craft of Poetry" seminar.

5. *The Poems of William Carlos Williams: A Critical Study* (Middletown, Conn., 1964), p. 11.

6. Notes from "The Craft of Poetry" seminar.

7. Ossman, p. 75.

8. Notes from "The Craft of Poetry" seminar.

9. From tapes made of Levertov's reading at University of Michigan, Ann Arbor, 1963.

10. Notes from "The Craft of Poetry" seminar.

11. "Monster with Melopoeia," p. 618.

12. "Olga Poems," *Poetry,* CVI, Nos. 1-2 (April-May 1965), 81-89.

Chapter Six

1. Notes from "The Craft of Poetry" seminar.

2. *Ibid.*

3. *Ibid.*

4. *Ibid.*

5. Taken from Miss Levertov's personal worksheets of the "Olga Poems," as are the rest of the excerpts used.

6. Notes from "The Craft of Poetry" seminar.

7. Microfilmed worksheets from the Poetry Collection, Lockwood Memorial Library, State University of New York at Buffalo, as are the rest of the excerpts from "A Sequence."

8. Notes from "The Craft of Poetry" seminar.

9. *Ibid.*

Chapter Seven

1. Personal letter to Dr. Williams dated June 18, 1962, p. 2. From the Yale University Library American Literature Collection, Dr. Williams' letters.

2. Statement accompanying poem chosen for *Poet's Choice,* ed. Paul Engle and Joseph Langland (New York, 1962), p. 211.

3. Notes from "The Craft of Poetry" seminar.

4. This attitude is understandable, since Levertov wrote most of these poems when she was nineteen, twenty, or twenty-one. The book was not published, however, until she was twenty-three.

5. *The Double Image* (London, 1946), p. 22.

6. *The Paris Review,* No. 33 (Winter-Spring, 1965), 37.

7. "O Taste and See," *Christian Science Monitor* (July 30, 1964), p. 5.

8. "Poets of the Given Ground," p. 252.

9. *Ibid.*

10. "Tribute to Jack Gilbert," *Genesis West,* I, No. 1 (Fall, 1962), 72.

11. "'An Order That Will Sing,'" *The Nation,* CXCII (May 13, 1961), 417.

12. "Monster with Melopoeia," p. 619.

13. "Things, Voices, Minds," *The Yale Review,* LII, No. 2 (Autumn, 1962), 129.

14. Edward Burroughs' interview with Miss Levertov for Station WUOM, Ann Arbor, Michigan. May, 1962.

15. "H.D.: An Appreciation," p. 183.

16. From notes for her introduction to the poetry reading of Robert Creeley, Robert Duncan, and herself at the Guggenheim Museum, New York, in April 1964.

17. *Ibid.*

18. *Ibid.*

19. Notes for "The Craft of Poetry" seminar.

Selected Bibliography

PRIMARY SOURCES

1. Poetry

"As It Happens" (poem), *The Paris Review*, No. 33 (Winter-Spring, 1965), 36.

The Double Image. London: The Cresset Press, 1946.

"Five Poems," *Quarterly Review of Literature*, XIII, Nos. 1, 2 (1965), 145-49. Includes "The Earth Worm," "Face to Face," "Thirst Song," "The Unknown," and "Snow Incense."

"The Goddess" and following statement, *Poet's Choice*, eds. PAUL ENGLE and JOSEPH LANGLAND. New York: The Dial Press, 1962.

Here and Now. San Francisco: City Lights Books, 1957.

The Jacob's Ladder. Norfolk, Conn.: New Directions, 1961.

"A Lamentation" (poem), *The Paris Review*, No. 33 (Winter-Spring, 1965), 37.

"Life at War" (poem), *Poetry*, CVIII, No. 3 (June, 1966), 149-51.

"The Mutes" (poem), *The Paris Review*, No. 33 (Winter-Spring, 1965), 38-39.

New British Poetry, ed. KENNETH REXROTH. Norfolk, Conn.: New Directions, 1948.

O Taste and See. Norfolk, Conn.: New Directions, 1964.

"Olga Poems," *Poetry*, CVI, Nos. 1-2 (April-May, 1965), 81-89.

Overland to the Islands. Highlands, North Carolina: Jargon Press, 1958.

"Six Vaishnava Lyrics," trans. with EDWARD C. DIMOCK, JR., *Poetry*, CVII, No. 3 (December, 1965), 176-181.

"The Son," *North American Review*, II (May, 1965), 54-5.

With Eyes at the Back of Our Heads. Norfolk, Conn.: New Directions, 1960.

2. Essays

"An Admonition," *things*, No. 1 (Fall, 1964), 4-7.

"An Approach to Public Poetry Listenings," *The Virginia Quarterly Review*, XLI, No. 3 (Summer, 1965), 422-33.

" 'The Arena Where We Fight,' " *The Nation*, CXCVII (December 21, 1963), 440-41.

"Distinct and Rum," *The Nation*, CXCIII, No. 8 (September 16, 1961), 166-67.

Introduction to Russell Edson's *The Very Thing That Happens*. Norfolk, Conn.: New Directions, 1964.

"Tribute to Jack Gilbert," *Genesis West*, I, No. 1 (Fall, 1962), 72.

"The Goddess" and following statement, *Poet's Choice*, eds. PAUL ENGLE and JOSEPH LANGLAND. New York: The Dial Press, 1962.

"H.D.: An Appreciation," *Poetry*, C (June, 1962), 182-86.

"Monster with Melopoeia," *The Nation*, CC, No. 23 (June 7, 1965), 618-19.

"Necessary Poetry," *Poetry*, XCVII (November, 1960), 102-9.

"A Note on the Work of the Imagination," *New Directions 17* (1961), 48-50.

"One of the Lucky," *The Nation*, CXCVI, No. 1 (April 13, 1963), 310-11.

"'An Order That Will Sing,'" *The Nation*, CXCII, No. 19 (May 13, 1961), 417-18.

"Play with Words," *The Nation*, CXCVIII, No. 6 (February 3, 1964), 126.

"Poets of the Given Ground," *The Nation*, CXCIII, No. 14 (October 14, 1961), 251-53.

"Rhythms of Speech," *New York Times Book Review* (June 21, 1964), 10-12.

"Some Notes on Organic Form," *Poetry*, CVI, No. 6 (September, 1965), 420-25.

"To Write Is To Listen," *Poetry*, CV (February, 1965), 326-29.

"What Is a Prose Poem?" *The Nation*, CXCIII, No. 22 (December 23, 1961), 518-19.

"William Carlos Williams," *The Nation*, CXCVI, No. 11 (March 16, 1963), 230.

3. *Unpublished Work*

"The Craft of Poetry," notes for a seminar taught during the winter of 1964-1965 at the 92nd Street Poetry Center, New York City.

Interview with Edward Burroughs, Station WUOM, Ann Arbor, Michigan; taped, 1962.

Microfilms of Miss Levertov's worksheets, Lockwood Memorial Library Poetry Collection, State University of New York at Buffalo, Buffalo, New York.

Private correspondence with Miss Levertov, 1963-1965.

Reading at University of Michigan, Ann Arbor, Michigan, 1962; and at University of British Columbia, Vancouver, British Columbia, Canada, 1963.

Selected Bibliography

Letters to William Carlos Williams. Yale University Library, American Literature Collection of Dr. Williams' letters.

Worksheets for "Olga Poems," Miss Levertov's personal collection.

University of British Columbia lectures and participation in panels held during poetry seminar, July-August, 1963.

SECONDARY SOURCES

ALLEN, DONALD M. (ed.). *The New American Poetry*, 1945-1960. New York: Grove Press, 1960. Contains poems as well as Levertov's statement on poetics and a biographical note by the poet.

BOWERING, GEORGE. "Blaser and Levertov," *Tish* (June, 1965), pp. 5-6. Considers Levertov a fine poet for her enduring "feminine grace" and the sensual strength evident in *O Taste and See*.

BUBER, MARTIN. *Tales of the Hasidim, Early and Late Masters*. New York: Schocken Books, 1947.

CAMBON, GLAUCO. "Nuovi poeti americani," *Verri*, VI, 1 (1962), 59-72. Sees Levertov as influenced by Williams and Marianne Moore, but good in her own right.

CARRUTH, HAYDEN. "Four New Books," *Poetry*, XCIII (November, 1958), 107-16. A favorable review of *Overland to the Islands*.

————. "An Informal Epic," *Poetry*, CV (January, 1965), 259-61. Sees Levertov as a "pastoral artist," a creator of universal "epics."

CORRINGTON, WILLIAM. "Incontestably dull," *Midwest*, Nos. 5-6 (Spring, 1963), 14-16. Describes Levertov's work as having "flat image and undistinguished phrase."

CREELEY, ROBERT. "*Here and Now*," *New Mexico Quarterly*, XXVII (Spring, 1957), 125-27. States that all of Levertov's work relates to "how to live."

DAVIS, BETTY MILLER. "Looking at the Thing," *Prairie Schooner* (Winter, 1962), 364-65. Survey of Levertov as "an extremely apt pupil of W. C. Williams."

ECKMAN, FREDERICK. *Cobras and Cockle Shells: Modes in Recent Poetry*. Flushing, New York: The Sparrow Press, 1958. Places Levertov as a "modernist" poet of high promise.

————. "Total individual responsibility," *Midwest*, Nos. 5-6 (Spring 1963), 16-19. Sees in this discerning review of *The Jacob's Ladder* a return to "humanitas," to the joy of personal responsibility.

FITTS, DUDLEY. "Separate Voices," *New York Times Book Review* (February 19, 1961), 36. Thinks Levertov is a poet with promise, though her subject matter seems very limited to him.

GARRIGUE, JEAN. *"With Eyes at the Back of Our Heads," Chelsea,* VII (May, 1960), 110-12. Rejects Levertov's work because her themes are too personal.

GOODMAN, PAUL. "The International Word," *The Nation,* CXCIV, 16 (April 21, 1962), 357-60. Considers Levertov as particularly concerned with mankind.

GUNN, THOM. "Things, Voices, Minds," *The Yale Review,* LII, No. 2 (Autumn 1962), 129-30. Sees Levertov as "fully individual," with a talent that is "considerable and still expanding."

HARTMAN, GEOFFREY. "Les Belles Dames Sans Merci," *Kenyon Review* (Autumn, 1960), 691-92. At her best, Levertov a classicist; at her weakest, an imitator of Pound.

HOWARD, RICHARD. "Comment," *Poetry,* CI (March, 1963), 412-18. Thinks Levertov is restricting herself too much to Imagist modes.

IGNATOW, DAVID. "Williams' Influence: Some Social Aspects," *Chelsea,* XIV (January, 1964), 154-61. Finds Levertov the closest poet to Williams theoretically, but with unifying virtues of her own.

JARRETT, EMMETT. "Always in the Garden," *Secant,* II, 2 (September, 1965), 8-10. Divides Levertov's poetry into the mystical-dream and the factually experienced. Finds both kinds strong.

JOHN, GODFREY. *"O Taste and See," Christian Science Monitor* (July 30, 1964), p. 5. Compares Levertov to Tagore in her sensitivity to daily life.

Judaism and Christianity: Essays presented to the Rev. Paul Philip Levertoff, D.D. London: J. B. Shears and Sons, 1939.

KENNEDY, X. J. "Fresh Patterns of Near Rhymes," *New York Times Book Review* (April 29, 1962), pp. 29-30. Points out Levertov's use of near-rhyme and assonance as an overlooked strength.

KUNITZ, STANLEY. "Process and Thing: A Year of Poetry," *Harpers* (September 1960), 102ff. Sees Levertov as "an original" among the mass.

LASK, THOMAS. "The Voice of the Poet," *New York Times Book Review* (December 2, 1962), p. 7. Finds Levertov always in "control."

LAUTER, PAUL. "Poetry Demanding and Detached," *New Leader* (May 15, 1961), pp. 22-23. Likes Levertov's poems for their honesty and their well-used rhetoric.

MARTZ, LOUIS L. "Recent Poetry: The Elegaic Mode," *The Yale Review,* LIV (December, 1965), 287-89. Finds Levertov writing in the contemplative vein of Wordsworth, more often of country than of city—except for occasional "beatnik" intrusions.

MAZZOCCI, ROBERT. "Three Poets," *New York Review of Books,* III

(December 31, 1964), 19. Considers Levertov's poems uneven, the unsuccessful work being too fragmentary, too personal, too banal.

MILLS, RALPH, JR. "Denise Levertov: Poetry of the Immediate," *Tri-Quarterly*, IV, 2 (Winter, 1962), 31-37. The best single article to date on Levertov's poetry.

—————. *Contemporary American Poetry*. New York: Random House, 1965. Contains a chapter on Denise Levertov, placing her in the contemporary scene and expanding on Mr. Mills' 1962 article, pp. 176-196.

MORSE, SAMUEL F. "A Baker's Dozen," *The Virginia Quarterly Review* (Spring, 1962), p. 324. Treats Levertov briefly but favorably.

NAPIER, JOHN. "A Brace of Beatniks," *Voices*, No. 174 (January-April, 1961), 48-49. Terms Levertov's poetry "dead." Napier's objections are largely to content.

OSSMAN, DAVID (ed.). *The Sullen Art*. New York: Corinth Books, 1963. Contains an interview with Levertov concerning the art of poetry, pp. 73-76.

PACK, ROBERT. "To Each Man His Own Muse," *Saturday Review* (December 8, 1962), pp. 26-29. Considers Levertov's strengths as her language and her use of the mystic; her weakness, as a tendency toward sentimentality.

PARKINSON, THOMAS. "*With Eyes at the Back of Our Heads*," *San Francisco Chronicle* (February 28, 1960), p. 22. Favorable.

REXROTH, KENNETH. "The Influence of French Poetry on American." *Assays*. Norfolk, Conn.: New Directions, 1961. Sees the impact of French poetry on Levertov, Creeley, and others as slight. In "The New Poetry," pp. 184-95, sees Levertov and Robert Duncan as the best of the new poets. In "Poets, Old and New," pp. 206-39, more praise for Levertov.

—————. "Levertov and the Young Poets," *New Leader* (July 9, 1962), pp. 21-22. Considers Levertov the leader of American poetry toward world literature, through her "humanity." Speaks of her work as "art as reconciliation."

—————. "The Poetry of Denise Levertov," *Poetry*, XCI (November, 1957), 120-23. Highly favorable review of *Here and Now*.

ROSENTHAL, M. L. "In Exquisite Chaos," *The Nation*, CLXXXVII (November 1, 1958), 324-27. Favorable commentary on Levertov's poems.

—————. *The Modern Poets: A Critical Introduction*. New York: Oxford University Press, 1960. Places Levertov within the Olson group, of which "absolute immediacy and spontaneity is the chief strength."

————. "Seven Voices," *The Reporter*, XXVIII, 1 (January 3, 1963), 46. Heavy emphasis on the Eichmann poem and "A Sequence."

SIMON, JOHN. "More Brass than Enduring," *Hudson Review* (Autumn, 1962), p. 455. Sees Levertov as a disciple of Williams and damns the work of both.

SIMPSON, LOUIS. "A Garland for the Muse," *Hudson Review* (Summer, 1960), pp. 289-90. Likes Levertov's work but would like to see her range of interests broadened.

SMITH, RAY. *"With Eyes at the Back of Our Heads," Library Journal*, LXXXV (March 1, 1960), 964. Likes Levertov's attainment of "ease and poise without affectation."

SORRENTINO, GILBERT. "Measure of Maturity," *The Nation*, CXCIV (March 10, 1962), 220-21. Sees new maturity of technique in *The Jacob's Ladder*.

STEPANCHEV, STEPHEN. *American Poetry since 1945*. New York: Harper and Row, 1965. Chronological survey of Levertov's work.

SUTTON, WALTER. "A Conversation with Denise Levertov," *The Minnesota Review*, V, 3-4 (December, 1965), 322-38.

SUPERVIELLE, JULES. *Selected Writings*. Norfolk, Conn.: New Directions, 1965. Partially translated by Levertov.

TRIEM, EVE. "Three Poets," *Poetry*, XCVI (August, 1960), 316-17. High praise for Levertov's inventive use of traditional devices.

TSVETAEVA, MARINA. "Five Poems," *The Russian Review*, XXIII, 2 (April, 1964), 131-35. Translated by Levertov.

WALDEN, ELIZABETH. *"O Taste and See," Library Journal*, LXXXIV (September 15, 1964), 3319. Impressed by Levertov's sensitivity to the immediate.

WICKES, FRANCIS G. *The Inner World of Choice*. New York: Harper and Row, 1963. Good insight into Jungian thought.

WRIGHT, JAMES. "Gravity and Incantation," *The Minnesota Review*, II (Spring, 1962), 424-27. Considers Levertov one of the best living poets, particularly for her prosody.

Index

Index

Index